Going for It!

THIRTY-SIX VIEWS ON THE GOOD LIFE

Edited by Carol S. Lawson

 CHRYSALIS BOOKS

West Chester, Pennsylvania

THE CHRYSALIS READER is a book series that examines themes related to the universal quest for wisdom. Inspired by the Swedenborg Foundation journal *Chrysalis,* each volume presents original short stories, essays, poetry, and art exploring the spiritual dimensions of a chosen theme. Works are selected by the series editor. For information on future themes or submission of original writings, contact Carol S. Lawson, Editor, Route 1, Box 184, Dillwyn, Virginia 23936.

LIBRARY OF CONGRESS CATALOGING-IN-PUBLICATION DATA
Going for It!: thirty-six views on the good life / edited by Carol S. Lawson
        p.   cm. — (Chrysalis reader: v. 4)
    ISBN 0-87785-337-0
    1.Conduct of life. 2 Spiritual life. I. Lawson, Carol S. II Series
BJ1581.2.G56   1997
810.8`0353—dc21   97-18274
                                                                        CIP

 **CHRYSALIS BOOKS**

Swedenborg Foundation, Publishers
320 North Church Street
West Chester, Pennsylvania 19380

Contents

"Thou Silver Moon with Silver Gleam"

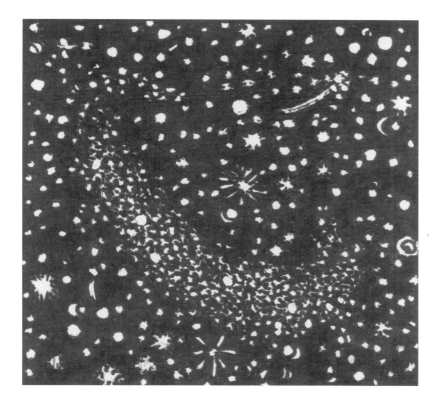

Carolyn Judson.
Pen-and-ink, 1987

SO SANG FRANCIS OF ASSISI in praising the natural order of the universe—its system of planets, creatures, flowers, fruits, and the spirit that to the saint seemed to encourage all living things to prosper beneath "burning sun with golden beam." When we stop to think today about how we are spending our lives, it is still the faraway silver gleam most of us reach for—the possibility that we can live the Good Life, a life of meaning. This book is about our current search for that ideal—the going in and the coming back—the spirit of adventure, the feckless moment, the meteor shower that plunges us past the edge of what is known.

IN THE 1960s AND 70s, it became apparent to many people that America's prosperity was not buying the Good Life. Some left the city for an earthier life in the country. In turning away from our postwar materialism, these pioneers broke in various ways with prevailing traditions. The individual lifetime described in Only One Life, the introduction to this book, represents just one of those 1970s breakers-of-tradition and seekers of truth.

The Reader moves us through four clusters of conditions encountered when reaching for the faraway ideal—the silver gleam—of lives meaningfully spent. Phase one is like waiting for those seldom-seen days in Alaska (described in the "Search for Gold") when the sun comes out, and the mining expert can take off on his search. The prospect of an environmental ethic that will preserve natural habitats and resources is fundamental to the Good Life; Tom Williams makes an assay from the first Earth Day to the current state of the world watch. Phase two is the voyage out to the unknown, accompanied by nerve-wracking solitude because you are the only one who can do what needs to be done. Abigail Calkins in Cameroon travels out in complete isolation; Margot Schilpp's lonely voyage is entirely inward, albeit to Uxmal, Egypt, Japan. The third phase is what you do in life with the cards dealt you: like the little girl in the Sky Meadow story who opened her arms and heart, letting out the magnificent female giant to rescue her from disaster, the very giant that had been within and available to the child always. And in the fourth phase, you see that in the composite experiences of a lifetime there is alchemical order—nothing is wasted.

Like Saint Francis, the writers of this book praise the universe. Its very *livingness* powers belief that whatever determination may be required to protect our community and to prosper our talents during this grand spinning voyage—is already there for us, inherently part of the sysem. According to these writers' stories, poems, and essays, the prerequisite to developing meaningful lives is the will and determination to make the effort to go for it!

Only One Life

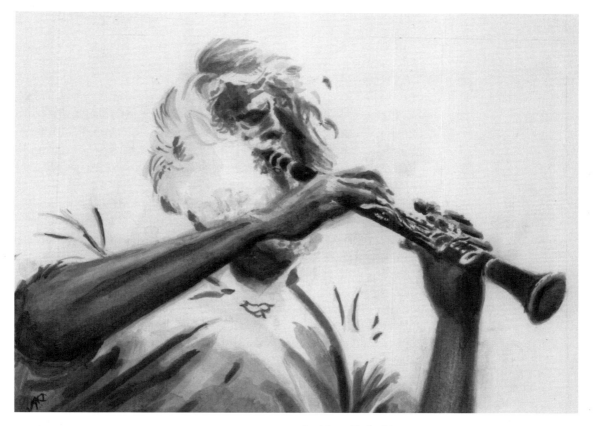

IN THE BACK OF HIS HENRY STREET BARBER SHOP in New York City, Papa wrote short stories of life on the Lower East Side and became a favorite of Abraham Cahan, editor of the *Jewish Daily Forward* where Papa's stories appeared. Papa was known as the O'Henry of Yiddish literature. As a youngster I wanted to become a writer too. (Somehow the way eluded me until the shock that eventually brought me to a lengthy sojourn in Mexico triggered curious stirrings that produced an occasional poem, many aphorisms, and heartfelt correspondence.) When my own children were youngsters, I talked so much about Papa that they thought they had known him even though he had died more than ten years before they were born. Once when I had wanted to take a speed-reading course, Papa asked, "Why do you want to read so fast? It takes me so long to write a story." It has taken me fifty years.

Dian McCarthy.
Saul Ader Playing the Clarinet.
Ink wash, 1997.

Know there is a door; be the door; open.

This becomes that moment I see that that is this.

TEN HIGH SCHOOL LESSONS ON THE CLARINET and an uncle's influence and suddenly I was in the New York University music department, thrust into harmony and counterpoint, of which I'd never heard. A C in that course and I knew I was not cut out to be a music major. At a loss, I thumbed through the NYU catalog; ignorant attraction to another strange word, _psychology,_ foretold my future. After three years of World War II in the Navy, I was later able to emerge from graduate school a psychoanalytic psychologist, a calling I came to love. But I have never lost my love for playing music and feel much satisfaction in my son Peter being an award-winning flutist with the Santa Fe Opera Company.

IN 1946 LEDA LIVANT AND I MARRIED, she the granddaughter of Joel Enteen, highly regarded Yiddishist, theater critic, founder of The Yiddish Folkshule, translator of Ibsen into Yiddish, and close friend to Ben Gurion. He and my father, Morris Aderschlager, knew one another.

In 1950 I began my professional training and my own psychoanalysis with a wonderful woman, Bertha Tumarin, whom I will remember forever. She along with my parents remain my most significant mentors, teaching me to be me.

Civilization does not feel like home.

BY 1970 LEDA AND I HAD TWO CHILDREN, Wendy, eighteen, and Peter, fifteen. We lived in Westport, Connecticut, a far cry from my unsophisticated and less elegant beginnings. That summer Leda and I, without the children, vacationed in Provincetown on Cape Cod. Alone with each other we found ourselves able to confront and painfully acknowledge that, as maverick as we thought we were, our lives had become constricted. We both yearned to be released from invisible chains that we did not understand. We wanted to find something. We didn't know what. We were frightened. We were angry. In that difficult time of beginning self exploration I wrote the following letter to my children:

> _Dear Wendy and Peter,_
> _This has been a very unusual time for Mom and me. Don't be_
> _surprised if when we come home there will be changes._
> _And thank you for being our teachers._
> _Love, Dad._

Leda and I wanted only to simplify our lives. We had no idea how the parameters of our lives were beginning to stretch, nor what form that stretching would take.

The second week of that vacation was in a shack on the water in the Indian Neck section of Wellfleet, also on the Cape. The first week's experience had begun to shatter us. It was scary but strangely it felt welcome. I spent much of the second week lying in the low tide, the strong sunlight flooding me with unbelievable visions. Such was the power of what Leda and I were confronting. I danced with rainbows in delectable dimensions I'd never dreamed of and everything was tumbling over everything.

Peter and his friends arrived to take over the shack for the third week after Leda and I left for home. There was an overlap of about an hour. In that hour came one of the most transforming moments of my life. Peter climbed out of the car. He stood on the sand facing his father with the sun pouring down on both of us. Then Peter hesitantly dared to break the silence:

> *Dad . . . are you really going to make changes? . . . I think so. . . . That's neat . . . now you can open up a candy store the way you always wanted. Well, maybe . . . or maybe I could become a shoemaker. . . . No, Dad. You should work with wood. You love wood. Dad . . . do you remember what I told you five years ago? No. What did you tell me five years ago? . . . Five years ago I told you it was a crime for you to be charging money for the kind of work you do! Whew! No, I don't remember. But I sure wish I did. That's okay Dad. I knew you'd come around!*

Our marriage had always seemed good. Some may continue to think ill of what we did. Its ending was not deliberate. It was as though we had no choice. So, shocking to many including myself, the way we found to a more simple, more honest way of being cost a great deal and was at odds with "responsible mores." In the intense pain of questioning the "success" of our marriage, we ended it. Scars remain. I miss what we had. I remember who I was. I know a little better who I am.

Leda moved to Provincetown and another relationship to find herself. Soon Mexico discovered me. Were we crazy to leave the children? Probably! Left alone with them I took the risk and shared with Wendy and Peter who were both now young adults that if I moved to Mexico I would no longer be able to support them, that each year I would be able to give them each a thousand dollars, and for the time being the house was theirs. I asked what they thought. They hurt deeply but in unison sang out, "Go for it, Dad!"

With these ambivalent blessings and with hopes that one day my head would clear, for the next two years each evening I stood on the roof of my tiny adobe house in San Miguel de Allende, facing northeast to Leda and Wendy and Peter, and wept.

Only while
standing
on my head
I discover that
up is down.

At transformation
the force of darkness
turns on itself
and catapults
to light.

Reveal a truth
and some will say
you need glasses.

Yes to everything, no to everything else.

I AM UNSURE WHEN THE CRISIS that brought me to Mexico led to revelations. I do know for sure that in moving to Mexico I headed for dramatic changes. Beginning with Mexico I entered my own real graduate school. Buddhism, Taoism, Hinduism, influences of Krishna Murti and Alan Watts and Ramana Marashi crossed my path and spirituality emerged. Meditation became a way to stillness and a way for Papa's eyes to become one with my own. I began to experience the feel of the stretching of my soul.

Years later one evening as dark approached I was on a park bench in the jardin of San Miguel. Something made me look up.

"You don't remember me," he said.

It was the Zapoteco Indian, Don José. His thin figure was slightly bent, silhouetted in the twilight, a sack over his shoulder holding his sparse belongings. We embraced.

Don José stayed with me in my house for many days teaching me much. I do not remember what he taught me. He said I would not remember but that he had put his teachings inside me and they would guide me whenever I needed. Maybe he was some kind of wandering shaman. He ate little, slept outside in the garden. One day Don José disappeared. I never saw him again. Until this writing I have rarely thought of him. He said it would be that way.

Wendy and Peter visited me in Mexico. Though miles and cultures apart, we remained close and in touch. I was there for them and they for me. Over the years rough edges that needed understanding have been attended. Leda and I also remained marginally in touch. Attempts to deal with our closeness, past or present, meet with resistance and remain unspoken. Nevertheless, on my fiftieth birthday Leda sent me a beautiful shawl from her loom with a note that read, "Does September happen in Mexico too?" Both our birthdays are in September. To this day, years later, the shawl remains part of my daily life as it drapes the large armchair I sit in when I counsel those who seek me out.

IN THAT THIRD QUARTER OF MY LIFE, in the depths of emotional despair from the disintegration of my family, my soul seemed to grow wings to escape those shadows. I played jazz wherever I went, and my sporadic writing began to take form. Eventually I sold my Westport house, and four of us, Wendy and I and our friends, Dennis and Margie, went farm hunting. On Prince Edward Island's rolling green hills, with other folks from all over the globe, we formed a community we called The Lost Dog Community. John Jiler and his beagle Jake hitchhiked from Chicago to visit us for three days and remained three years as the fifth member of our farm family. All of us had descended on Prince Edward Island to buy abandoned farms. Dennis named ours Spruce Meadow Farm. We had one-hundred-thirty acres, seventy-five cleared and the rest Spruce forest, two streams, a barn, chicken house that Dennis converted into a honey house, carpenter shop, woodhouse for twenty cords of firewood, and a great eleven-room house—no plumbing or electricity. How much? Nine thousand dollars. We had great friends. We had great times. We raised grain and vegetables and three acres of organic strawberries and tended fifty beehives.

Deep in the woods, in the early stages of our farm, with Margie's help, I fashioned a small cabin with salvaged lumber and timber from demolished old farm buildings. With every nail, each screw and bolt, and each piece of hand-cut lumber tailored to fit, lumber became a consuming love affair. Little did I know that this simple, sturdy, impeccable work of art would one day become my sacred hermitage, my dream come true. If not for Wendy it would never have happened, as I will explain later.

At the farm Leda wrote to me from Greece that the studio she shared in Provincetown was vacant until her return. Would I like to make use of it? Wendy and Dennis needed space and privacy, without me, to work out their personal life. It felt right to leave the farm.

IN PROVINCETOWN I FOUND A HAVEN for my healing. I have now lived here many years. From Provincetown Margie left for California and our five-year intimate relationship ground to an unwanted halt. I have lived alone since. Soon I found this studio where I continue my reclusive life. By this time Leda had, a year or so before, returned from Greece and moved on to Arizona. Interesting, my studio is on the same street as Leda's was. The number of her studio was 22. Mine is 11. Everything, but everything, needed to equip my new abode flew to me from nowhere and everywhere without asking. From the street, from the dump, from yard sales everything appeared.

One day my attention was drawn to two armchairs I had acquired. They sat opposite each other in front of the fireplace. Was I getting ready to return to work? Sure enough. The next day on a walk down Commercial Street a young man rolled out of the Foc'sle Bar and pleaded with me to help him with his life. I explained I didn't practice psychotherapy any more but would be glad to talk informally with him on the street. It wasn't an argument, but whatever it was he won. He became my first appointment after a self-imposed eight-year sabbatical. He came. He sat in one of the armchairs. I sat in the other one, the one with Leda's shawl draped around it. When the session was over the young man asked what was my fee? *That's*

Every you
is a truth,
the holy truth,
so help you God.

The emptied mind makes room for the soul.

okay Dad, I knew you'd come around! . . . I heard myself say "There is no fee . . ." and that's the way it has been since.

The nature of my work too had transformed to *Conversations with Saul: A Spiritual / Human Dialogue.* It invites those who come for counsel to enter their own realm of stillness where, I believe, ancient wisdoms dwell and can be found only by learning to listen.

Wendy was the only one of the original four from Spruce Meadow Farm to remain on Prince Edward Island. When she left the farm she moved to Charlottetown, raised her daughter, managed matters of the farm until it got sold, and she nurtured and trained herself to become a professional for the Canadian Broadcasting Company.

Did you ever notice whether the tide's comin' or goin', the water's always comin'.

Years later a telephone call from Wendy:

Dad, the new owners of the farm want to pay off the mortgage ahead of time. What do you think? . . . Let them. . . . Maybe I could swing a deal. . . . What kind of deal? . . . I could tell them okay if they let me take your cabin off the farm . . . You could do that? . . . I'll be firm and make that the condition.

There is no more perfect than now.

And she did. With devotion, knowing what the cabin meant to me, after the potato harvest she arranged to have the cabin hoisted onto a flatbed truck and moved fifty miles to a swell piece of land on Howe Point in the woods, by the sea, a mile from nearest neighbors.

The snow plow clears the highway and violates the snow.

And so, as I entered what could become the fourth quarter of my life, I began taking summer leave from the haven of Provincetown, where in summer frantic civilization makes its invasion, and I head north for the heaven of Prince Edward Island. My cabin is called *Hermitage de Quietude Circa del Mar.* Here those who seek counsel, old and new, find me in the stillness of myself. Occasional writing, such as these brief scenes of my life with aphorisms, spins out of me as I live away from the mainstream of the world and close to the mainstream of my soul.

Born in 1921, SAUL ADER was raised in the Catskill Mountains and New York City with parents who had emigrated from Eastern Europe. College was New York University. Graduate schools included the New School for Social Research and Yale University. The illustration of Saul at his cabin is by Dian McCarthy (ink wash, 1997).

Going for It!

THIRTY-SIX VIEWS ON THE GOOD LIFE

PART I

Waiting for an Opening

Peter and his friends arrived to take over the shack for the third week after Leda and I left for home. There was an overlap of about an hour. Peter climbed out of the car. He stood on the sand facing his father with the sun pouring down on both of us.

PHILOSOPHERS, THEOLOGIANS, AND ORDINARY PEOPLE who love to think, continually define one or another pattern in human living that accounts for all the subtle variations of human experience. *Going for It!* implies one of these perennial philosophies, illustrating four stages—frustration, change, growth, and transformation—that anyone may recognize as a pattern in our lives.

These parts of this volume closely follow a fully articulated theory of psychological development, spiritual growth, and theological rebirth, formulated by Emanuel Swedenborg. He described it as *Becoming New,* a process so universal in application that he found it illustrated in the Creation Story related in the first chapter of the first book of the Bible.

In that model, the Beginning—the situation from which the process starts—is barren and empty. It is a time in our living that may or may not seem bad, but certainly isn't good; a circumstance we will happily change as soon as someone shows us a better way, or we find a way out.

Waiting for an opening is painful without patience, but an opening awaited too patiently can be missed. These poems, Thomas Williams' analysis of our situation, Ralph Pray's wilderness recollections, and Patricia Shuetz' haunting fiction show how the opening is found through a restless, active kind of waiting, a seeking that is not limited to what we expect to find or think we want.

Winslow Homer.
The Nooning.
Oil on canvas, twentieth
century. Hartford,
Connecticut: Wadsworth
Atheneum. The Ella
Gallup Sumner
and Mary Catlin Sumner
Collection Fund.

The following author joined the newly-enacted federal air pollution program in 1957 when the problem was receiving little national attention. From 1957 through 1980, Tom Williams championed communication efforts—first in the Department of Health, Education, and Welfare, and later in the Environmental Protection Agency—to ensure that vital environmental data reached the public. Throughout his career in government, he and his coworkers also developed programs to encourage the involvement of environmental, health, civic, and service organizations in dealing with environmental problems. When Tom retired from this work, former senator and Secretary of State Edmund S. Muskie wrote: "If a history of the environmental movement is ever written, I am confident that your key role will be recognized. I know of no person who was more directly responsible for developing public interest and support for pollution control, and I know just how difficult that task appeared in the beginning. Our success is due in large part to your work."

Among a number of other commendations and awards Tom received were the Superior Service Award of the Department of Health, Education, and Welfare, and the Distinguished Career Award of the Enviromental Protection Agency. From his long-range perspective, Tom now summarizes environmental protection prospects on the threshold of a new century. He warns that the planet is at risk, but reminds us of our power. He suggests that there can be no Good Life on this earth if we fail to sustain our planet for ourselves and all future generations.

THOMAS F. WILLIAMS

Good for All or Good for None

WE MODERN HUMAN BEINGS with our astounding population growth and our wondrous technology are well on our way to making the earth unfit for human habitation. At some time between the fifty-thousand and one-hundred-thousand years ago when *Homo sapiens sapiens* (man the doubly wise) appeared until about 100 BCE there were never more than three million people on this planet. About 1,500 years after than, one billion, and by 1945, two billion. It has taken only fifty years to reach almost six billion, which is where we are now. Currently, we are adding a billion more people every decade, so by 2030, this planet, which does not grow, will be home to about nine billion people. Ninety-five percent of the increase will be in the developing world where 80 percent of the world's people live with only 20 percent of the world's income, where 1.2 billion have no access to drinkable water, where 2 billion are without electricity, and in which 40,000 people die each day from hunger-related disease. Among the many environmental problems which threaten *all* countries today are global warming, depletion of the ozone layer, of living species, of topsoil, and of fisheries, in addition to increasing deforestation and desertification and the widespread contamination of groundwater. It may be time to invent a new name for our species. While we have become a powerful geological force indeed, we have so far displayed very little wisdom in the process.

During the countless generations that preceded the Industrial Revolution, humans were hardly gentle caretakers of the environment, as some have romanticized. Pre-Columbian tribes and civilizations also created wastelands and deserts. But they lacked the scientific knowledge which has enabled us to create the truly global environmental problems that we face today. Population has exploded in step with our growing ability to control disease and with the triumph of fossil and nuclear-powered machines over wind and muscle. We have transformed the world's food system and made it dependent on nonrenewable resources, such as petroleum-based fertilizers, pesticides, herbicides, and, increasingly, on water pumped from underground aquifers.

The earth has always been subject to natural disturbances, ranging from fires and floods to cyclones and volcanos, but no natural cataclysm, aside from comets or the advance of glaciers, is capable of causing the degree of global damage with which we threaten ourselves today. A very serious problem our actions have created is global warming, often called the greenhouse effect.

Without the "normal" greenhouse effect, life on earth as we know it would not exist. Natural greenhouse gases include water vapor and carbon dioxide that form an atmospheric blanket about twelve miles thick, which traps nearly 90 percent of the infrared rays radiated from the earth back toward space, retaining them long enough to keep the earth's average temperature at about 60 degrees Fahrenheit. But we are interfering in dangerous ways with this vital process. Since the beginning of the industrial revolution we have been placing enormous amounts of carbon into the atmosphere through our increasing use of wood, coal, oil, and natural gas. In the atmosphere each atom of carbon combines with two atoms of oxygen to produce carbon dioxide. According to data obtained from the retrieval of ancient ice cores, the amount of carbon dioxide in the atmosphere has fluctuated between 200 parts per million during the last two ice ages and 300 parts per million during the period of great warming between the two ice ages. The global average temperature rose and fell in accordance with carbon dioxide measurements. We have outdone nature by pushing the level to 355 ppm, with most of the change since World War II. As the release of carbon to the atmosphere continues to exceed the uptake of carbon by the oceans and vegetation, we are courting disaster. According to the United Nations Panel on Climate Change, the global temperature is likely to increase between 1.8 and 6.3 degrees by the year 2100. At an increase of 3.6 degrees, the consequences would include a rise in sea level from one to three feet, more frequent and more violent storms, changes in rainfall patterns that would adversely affect agriculture, the inundation of coastal communities where more than half the world's population lives, and the likely spread of infectious diseases. As much as 10,000 square miles of our country's coastline would be submerged.

At the 1992 Earth Summit, 160 countries endorsed the United Nations Framework Convention on Climate Change. A primary goal was to establish greenhouse gas emissions at 1990 levels by the year 2000. In 1992, however, our government supported a voluntary, rather than a binding goal of reducing emissions to 1990 levels by the year 2000. It appears that only Great Britain and Germany may comply. At the 1996 International Climate Conference in Geneva, our state department set forth a proposal to seek binding limits on greenhouse gases after the year 2000. Despite the fact that the urgent need to curtail global emissions is backed by an international body made up of more than 2,000 of the world's best climate scientists, the President's decision prompted an angry response from domestic coal, oil, and utility industries. However, this should surprise no one since most of the environmental improvements proposed in the last forty years were scorned and fiercely resisted until public opinion prompted Congress to enact them into law.

Forests play a critical role in stabilizing global climate by absorbing carbon dioxide from the atmosphere and in regulating the hydrological cycle. They also provide the most prolific habitat for living species. Most critical of all are the tropical rain forests now threatened as never before. It is estimated that they contain at least half of all plant and animal species on earth—species which cannot survive anywhere else. Unlike temperate deciduous forests, rain forests are rooted in thin, poor soils. The far greater portion of the nutrients needed are in the forest itself. Consequently, when portions of them are destroyed to produce farmland, the farmer enjoys a very small short-term gain and the loss is incalculable and forever. Rain forests are in danger. They are being clear-cut for lumber, burned to produce pasture, and flooded by hydroelectric dams to generate power. Debts owed by developing countries to the industrialized nations encourage their careless exploitation. Massive and often inappropriate development projects, rapid population growth, and shortages of fuel contribute to the astounding prediction that at the current rate of deforestation, virtually all of these irreplaceable forests will have disappeared during the next century. We are a long way from identifying all the species of plants and animals they contain and from discovering their uses in medicine and other fields. Moreover, since forests absorb great amounts of carbon dioxide, a double contribution to global warming occurs when trees are cut down and burned. Yet, in August 1996, the Consultative Group on International Agricultural Research reported that 38.1 million acres of forest are lost every year. Poor farmers who destroy patches of forest to feed their families are responsible for 25 million acres of the annual loss.

The earth's surface is also being altered significantly by the misuse of drylands, which enlarges deserts. Like the poor farmers who diminish the forests, growing populations of nomadic peoples gather firewood and graze their herds, which denudes the land and invites the desert's advance. According to a United Nations study, over-exploitation is causing severe losses in productivity in 60 percent of the dry croplands and 80 percent of the dry rangelands.

Mountainous areas of the developing world are also endangered. Rapid population growth has led to cultivation of their thin soils which become highly vulnerable to erosion. Rivers which drain the mountains of rain and melted snow are filling up with silt that diminishes their capacity to carry the volumes of water they once transported. The result is serious flooding, which claims many lives, in addition to further reducing the amount of arable land.

Also of increasing concern is the loss of biological diversity that accompanies rising pollution levels and rapid conversion of virgin lands to human uses. Both plants and animals are being lost forever before we have had the chance to evaluate their potential contribution to new medical and other uses. Biodiversity loss narrows the gene pool that is critical to the cross breeding of wild plants with commercial species to improve yield and resistance to pests and disease.

The vast reach of our numbers and technology over the land has also profoundly affected the oceans of the world. Growth in cities, harbors, industrial installations, and increased pollution have destroyed coral reefs, wetland, and mangrove forests. Land-based sources contribute up to 90 percent of coastal pollution. More fishing vessels with new, more effective technology continue to pursue dwindling numbers of fish while coral mining and blast fishing accelerate the damage to ocean and coastal habitats. Fishing grounds once among the world's most productive are now essentially closed. Stocks of some large ocean fish have declined from 60 to 90 percent in the past two decades. The U.N. estimates that 70 percent of the world's important fish stocks are fully or over-exploited.

The American people have been supporting the modern environmental movement far longer and far more consistently than most of us realize. Contrary to widespread misguided opinion, the movement was not launched by Rachel Carson's excellent book, *Silent Spring*, in 1962, nor by college students during the first Earth Day in 1970. The real breakthrough began in the mid-1950s when the national news media began to give serious and sustained attention to the work of the federal air and water pollution programs of the U.S. Public Health Service, to the air pollution control efforts of Los Angeles County, and to the seminal legislative efforts of former Senator Edmund Muskie of Maine. The extraordinary degree of news media attention given to national conferences on air pollution in 1958, 1962, and 1966 also helped make inevitable the Earth Day observances and the creation of the Environmental Protection Agency in 1970.

Within our own borders we have made progress. Even though air pollution is still responsible for thousands of premature deaths each year, sulphur dioxide levels have been reduced by 40 percent since 1970, airborne lead by 90 percent, and carbon monoxide by 50 percent. These and other cuts have cost billions of dollars but have produced trillions of dollars in benefits to human health. Today almost two-thirds of the bodies of water in our country are safe for swimming and fishing. About one-third were considered safe twenty years ago. The creation of new toxic dumps has declined and increased recycling has lowered the amount of household trash dumped into landfills. It also appears that, at last, we are no longer dumping municipal sludge into the ocean. Nevertheless, much remains to be done to deal with current health problems as well as with the ugly remains of past neglect.

Recently there have been several encouraging signs which suggest that environmental problems are being taken more seriously on a global basis. At the annual meeting of the World Bank and International Monetary Fund in 1996, it was noted that 225 billion dollars were going to developing countries and that all of the loans are now affected by how proposals may affect the environment. The sum includes mutual and pension funds, investments by multinational corporations as well as by banks and other private institutions. In 1987 the amount was only 18.4 billion dollars. The growing amount of private investment now dwarfs the 55 billion that the World Bank and other official sources lent to developing nations in 1995. Nevertheless, scores of poor countries are still being left out because the bulk of private capital is flowing into about twenty nations, led by China, that offer attractive investment prospects.

An unprecedented development in our country's efforts to cope with global environmental problems occurred last year when the former U.S. Secretary of State, Warren Christopher, announced a new policy to integrate environmental concerns into our country's overall diplomacy and place them in the upper levels of U.S. security interests. He noted that disputes over water provoke international tensions and that population growth and diminishing resources can provoke mass migration, political upheaval, and conflict.

On April 22, 1997, Secretary of State Madeleine Albright, issued *Environmental Diplomacy,* the first of what will become "annual Earth Day reports to update global environmental challenges and policy developments and to set priorities for the coming year." In a letter accompanying the report, Vice President Gore states that the report "documents an important turning point in U.S. foreign policy—a change the President and I strongly support." Mr. Gore is the author of *Earth in the Balance,* published in 1992, which dealt with pollution, overpopulation, deforestation, global warming, and other major environental issues.

The first issue of *Environmental Diplomacy* contains a number of examples of the various ways in which our government is now assisting other countries in dealing with environmental problems. Following is a sampling of them.

A group of chemical compounds, including PCBs and DDT—though no longer used in our country—are still used abroad and continue to turn up in the fatty tissue of animals and people. Also known as persistent organic pollutants, these compounds are capable of traveling thousands of miles from their source. Many developing countries are not currently capable of effectively regulating their use. The United States and over a hundred other countries have begun negotiating a global agreement to ban the production of 12 of the most hazardous persistent organic pollutants on the planet.

China, which could surpass the United States as the largest consumer of energy by 2020, relies primarily on coal with inadequate attention to emissions. The result is high levels of sulfur in the air which cause acid rain in China and other countries in the region. Through a bilateral forum the U.S. is working to address the many problems posed by China's energy needs and to apply new technology in addressing them. We are also helping China to inventory its emissions of greenhouse gases and to upgrade its pulverized coal power to a more environmentally sound system.

The United States organized and is working through the global London Dumping Convention to reduce ocean dumping of waste and contaminants and through the U.N.'s International Maritime Organization to reduce vessel discharge.

The State Department is involved in helping countries around the world counter threats to their freshwater resources. One example involves India where 70 percent of surface water is polluted and waterborne diseases account for two thirds of all illnesses in the country. Under a U.S.–India agreement begun by the State Department in 1995, the U.S. Agency for International Development contributes $125 million in loan guarantees and provides technical assistance and training for the development and financing of commercially viable water supply, sewage, and wastewater treatment projects in India.

In Eastern Europe, where decades of reliance on coal-fired power plants with a lack of regulation have severely degraded air quality, the U.S. was instrumental in establishing the Regional

Environmental Center for Central and Eastern Europe to help develop and enforce air quality regulations.

During the summer of 1997, two important environmental issues were being hotly debated in our country. One is over regulations introduced by EPA last November to cut emissions of ozone and particulates, the other is over the U.S. role in the important Third Conference of the U.N. Framework Convention on Climate Change which will be held in Kyoto, Japan, this December. Both issues have generated what may be the most fierce and costly campaigns ever mounted by corporations and trade groups against environmental proposals.

Under EPA's current particulate standards, only particles 10 microns in diameter or larger are regulated. Under the new rules, particles as low as 2.5 microns in diameter would be covered. Research indicates that the smaller particles are responsible for causing or exacerbating respiratory illnesses that cause 15,000 deaths each year and billions of dollars in medical expenses. Opponents argue that the scientific evidence is not conclusive and that the new standards could hobble economic development. On June 25, 1997, President Clinton declared his support for the new regulations that will eventually force scores of cities to cut pollution or face sanctions. Standards on particulates would be delayed for five years to allow completion of a nationwide network. After that, cities would have at least another two years to devise a pollution-reduction strategy.

On June 27, 1997, the second United Nations Earth Summit ended five days of speeches and negotiations among nearly 180 countries, including 44 heads of state, without significant progress toward resolving any of the planet's environmental problems. There was none of the optimism that followed the original Earth Summit in Rio de Janeiro five years ago. Negotiators had hoped to reach consensus on timetables for the reduction of greenhouse gases, for firm commitments from developed countries to increase aid to developing countries for environmental efforts, and for a pact to protect forests.

Instead, the meeting was dominated by disputes between developed and developing countries and between the United States and Europe. The European Union favors reducing emissions at this time to a level 15 percent below the world's 1990 output. President Clinton promised only to support "realistic and binding limits" on emissions during the treaty to be signed in Kyoto in December.

In the end, negotiators were able to agree to only vague commitments to fight poverty, to increase aid to developing countries, and to future talks on preserving forests and curbing greenhouse emissions. All the hard work remains for the Third Conference of the

U.N. Framework Convention on Climate Change to be held in Kyoto, Japan, in December.

Current developments suggest that the meeting will not be easy for representatives from our country. U.S. coal, oil and motor vehicle interests are increasing their campaign to deny the need for change. Our Senate has expressed its sentiments by voting 95 to 0 against any agreement in Kyoto to reduce greenhouse gas emissions unless developing nations reduce theirs accordingly. Such a step at this time would be viewed as grossly unfair and could undermine the talks.

Nevertheless it is critical that the nations and negotiators do a better job in December than they did in June. As both population and global pollution continue to increase, mandatory cuts in carbon dioxide emissions from major industrial powers must be achieved. Our country with only 4 percent of the world's population produces 20 percent of the world's greenhouse gases—more than any other country. Without doubt, we have a major role to play in the international effort. We are also a major reason for hope among the billions who live in developing nations. The world wide scope of modern methods of communication encourages the poorest persons on the planet to aspire to "the good life" available to those who live in the developed nations. Their aspirations cannot be postponed indefinitely, and our country cannot play its proper role without sustained public support here at home. Can we fail? Of course, we can. Until recently in our nation's history, most of us were affected by what has been called a frontier mentality which favored rapid growth and development at almost any cost. We killed or forced onto reservations the Native Americans and practiced headlong exploitation of wildlife, forests, rivers, and virtually every other aspect of nature that was exploitable. And still among us today are many voters and politicians who remain in thrall to that obsolete viewpoint. It was only yesterday when members of the 104th Congress sought to unravel decades of environmental progress. Fortunately, they failed and some of them no longer represent us. One more example of the simple truth that it really is up to the people, and in this century, all of the races as well, to ensure that this planet remains a suitable place for life, liberty, and the pursuit of happiness.

LINDA PASTAN

April

The young cherry trees
stick out their limbs
as awkwardly as foals
standing for the first time.
Around them the maples
are itchy with new growth,
and dogwoods stand
in ballet poses.
How many leaves
open their green shutters now
to let April through.

A writer and lecturer at Breadloaf Writers Conference, LINDA PASTAN has received many awards for her work; these include a fellowship from the National Endowment for the Arts, the Dylan Thomas Poetry Award, and the di Castagnola Award. Her most recent book of verse, being published by Norton, is due out this year.

RALPH E. PRAY

The Search for Gold

Jenny McMaster.
Etching.

ON THOSE SELDOM-SEEN DAYS IN THIS REGION when the sun comes out, the inside passage of Alaska displays rare vistas that have been obscured by fog for weeks. Rainfall reaches 200 inches in some years. Sunny days thus would prompt me to lock the doors to the Alaska Territorial Assay Office and to venture alone into the far wilderness in my boat at high speed in my life-long search for gold. Earlier years had been spent preparing for the quest, studying and working at the assaying, mining, and metallurgy of the precious metal in well-known mines and colleges of the American West. Alaska's frontier became the forge which shaped my skills and individuality. The challenge to produce something useful to society from untouched regions went hand in hand with a concern for the undefended vastness and the impact mining activity might have on its grandeur.

My boat trip led from Ketchikan to all the land I could quickly reach by water. The arc of blue sky above me, the green adorning the land around me, the silvery darkness of the sea split by the arrow of the boat's white wake, lured me far from my home port. The forests I reached had no human footprints or memory of them. Deer and black bear roamed these woods. The gray wolf was present but seldom seen. Sounds were of wind whistling through tall treetops, of water rushing to reach the sea, of the loon's cry from its watery home, and of waves lapping against rocky beaches.

My only companion on these journeys was Duke, a Mackenzie husky of unfettered eagerness. With the boat beached or anchored nearby, Duke and I examined the exposed geology and rock along the shoreline. Inland exploration was hampered by the thick carpet of muskeg covering everything, including rock outcrops. The muskeg was a dense tangle of roots, vines, plants, bushes, leaves, and evergreen needles.

THE BANNER YEAR, THE YEAR OF MY FIND, was one of gradual, step-by-step success. The first indication was a pathfinder to gold rather than the mineral itself. I found pieces and chunks of white quartz on one bank of a river flowing into the salt water. Little vugs in the whiteness had a story to tell of former occupants long oxidized out of existence, departed metallic compounds often found with gold.

A mile into the Sitka spruce rain forest from the river, through devil's club thorny growth and fallen five-foot-thick rotting trees, I found pieces of native gold lying on the rock shelf beside a log-cluttered stream. The loose nuggets and flakes had washed down from the hillside or upstream. Pieces of accompanying white quartz identical to those along the river let me know a vein existed someplace between the two waterways.

That was also the day the new outboard engine froze tight with a mechanical defect on the way out of my harbor inlet. The boat was protected from the open sea, but we were without any means of going on from our extremely remote region. A wait for rescue by air, perhaps late the next day, was the only option. I paddled to shore using a cabin seat and tied up in darkness at high tide to a shoreline tree.

There were no night air flights. All aircraft were float planes and no waterway had lights. But at ten that night I heard, for the first time in the Alaska bush after dark, a small-engine plane.

It flew directly toward me like an arrow from heaven, wing-lights dimly visible. I had a three-cell flashlight and signaled three bursts repeatedly into the blackness. He circled. I continued flashing as he came down to land on the ocean water in the dark and taxied to my beached boat. The door flew open. Standing on the passenger float I lifted Duke into the cabin and followed to see a friendly pilot and a man on a stretcher in back. It was a mercy flight to Ketchikan General Hospital from a village on the Canadian border. Fifteen minutes later we landed on the sea beside the city in the gray haze of the street lights along the docks.

I towed my cruiser into town the next day with a friend's boat and replaced the engine with two new ones. That was the only caution. The memory of gold lying exposed in sight was so stimulating that sunlight was no longer a condition required for the trip across the water. My mind seemed to be a one-way boulevard going directly to the gold, with return an afterthought. Sleep was difficult on those nights when I couldn't get my mind away from the thought of a basketball-size collection of gold pieces worth a million dollars.

THE TRUE SEARCH WAS FOR THE SOURCE, the *mother lode* up the hill or upstream from the gold flakes that classically wash down the *placer.* The lode might contain gold worth millions, or tens or even hundreds of millions. But there was nothing to see except the bed of the thick, green forest. I criss-crossed the area through, under, and over every conceivable impasse, but found not a single window through the muskeg into white quartz terra firma.

Time after time, from the dry safety of civilization, I sped across the turbulent ocean to the discovery. During twenty-foot tides and with the Tongass Trading Company tidebook in my shirt pocket, I still let my boat get stranded on the beach or far out from shore rather than leave the search to reposition the anchor. One day the tide came in so far I had to either swim in the ice-cold water for my boat rope or wait hours for it to appear as the tide went out.

ONE EVENING I WAS STILL IN THE FOREST when the sky went black. I had a headlamp with a belt battery and was running Duke ahead in the beam as we climbed through the wet, dense growth and rock cliffs toward the boat. We were still a thousand feet from shore when the light bulb suddenly burned out. The darkness was total. It wasn't possible to proceed. Duke sat between my feet. Daylight was nine hours away, and there would be deep concern in the city if I wasn't back in two hours. On impulse, I reached up to the light banded on my head and snapped my thumb on the glass. The burned filament connected, welded, and gave forth a white light. It wasn't something I'd learned; I'd never heard of doing that before. We moved on instantly.

There seemed to be guidance, though nothing was expected. In my optimistic reach beyond prudence, I tested it. There was no limit. Every accident had an instant reprieve. Every mistake was corrected without loss. Every problem had a solution just behind it.

I was in the best world.

THE LAST DAY WAS THE DAY OF THE SYMBOL. Paths had been beaten into the forest floor by my many trips. The endless months of searching seemed to be futile. On this day I was near the crest of the hill between the river and the stream, still looking for the quartz vein, when I saw a recent tree-fall. Extremely large trees are sometimes blown down during storms. The entire root system comes up as the tree goes down. This was such a tree. The roots with dirt still clinging to them rose fifteen feet straight into the air, a thick mass of brown muskeg torn out of the ground draped across the trunk. I clambered up the jutting broken roots to stand near the top and get a good look at the surroundings—more of the same. I looked down at the huge hole the roots came out of.

There before me, in full sight, was the completely exposed white quartz vein!

Gold metal was visible on the surface in a series of small patches and a few big ones. It was rich, incredibly rich. The quartz vein was wide and as white as milk. I held onto the roots tightly as my legs lost their strength and the air whooshed from my lungs at the shock. The surface beneath the muskeg on each side of the vein had to be almost paved with gold pieces broken out of the rock during millions of freeze–thaw cycles while the lighter rock washed away. I climbed down into the hole and chipped the quartz around one of the large pieces of gold until it broke free.

That gold, saved for thirty years, is in the wedding rings of my children.

It was time to think. I could almost hear the melange of familiar sounds coming from gigantic diesel trucks, buzzing chain saws, chattering air drills, crashing trees, rock crushers, huge bulldozers, and thundering ball mills.

This earth shudder had not reached my Alaska.

On the way out I was walking beside the stream, deep in thought, when two bald eagles glided into my region. They were looking for salmon in the shallow waters. Both of the eagles were huge, with seven-foot wingspans, the female as usual was somewhat larger. The male spiraled above me, white-crowned head fastened to his search. I sat on the gravel bank beside the heavy growth to watch. Suddenly the female changed her search pattern and flew toward the river. The male descended majestically in a wide circle to seek a perch.

In the stillness of midday, the eagle settled on a top spruce branch, gripping it so tightly with encircled talons that shreds of bark came whispering down through the foliage to settle like rain on the muskeg below. He turned to look for his mate, and let out a great cry that pierced to the very backbone of my soul, *KAAAAAA!!!*

At that instant I became aware, suddenly and with vibrant force, of the embrace in which I existed, of the extensions granted my incautious life, of the conclusion to my quest.

Finding the gold had been a joyous shock, a moment of pure exhilaration. Whatever the gold orebody was worth I was prepared to spend in the next few minutes to purchase peace for this part of the best world. The months of looking for the gold were tokens of life's labor at learning the truth. I had just seen and heard that all of earth's objects, not only gold, were precious.

The cry of the eagle was holistically the ever-new and eternal purity in all the things its sound touched. How simple the lesson, a mere drop of truth in an ocean of ambition, a quick sight and sound symbolizing not just nature but the inside of all that exists.

RALPH PRAY holds degrees from the University of Alaska and the Colorado School of Mines and has traveled widely in his work in mineral-property evaluations. Dr. Pray has been writing for publication for thirty-nine years. The illustration is an etching by JENNY MCMASTER, Ottowa, who is majoring in art history and religion at Carleton University.

STEVEN LAUTERMILCH

Sleeping Muse

How she sleeps.

The eyes, like
almonds, the eyelids, like the shells
of almonds, sealed in sweetness—
the bass
clef of the ear, the
half note
of the mouth, the spear
points, laurel leaves of each lip,
pipes
of the nostrils
all awakening, just the
slightest, and still
barely visible, as if the music
taking form
within the rock
were being dropped,
dripping into her, not from outside, but
within—
from a body, so
vast, starfield and galaxy, it is invisible,
untouchable,—
only (like the breath
to one breathing, or a waking
kiss) having to be tasted
to be heard.

After twenty-one years of teaching at the University of North Carolina-Greensboro, STEVE LAUTERMILCH moved to the Outer Banks of North Carolina, where he now writes, photographs, and offers workshops in dream study, meditation, and writing. Steve's poem "Crane Suite" is being awarded first place in the 1997 River Oak Review Poetry Competition. His new book of poems, *Petals on a Burning Pond,* has just been published by Hour Press.

JUDITH ADAMS

Naturalization

Twenty six Amendments.
Bill of Rights. Who can
Start a War, who has the
Final nod of the Law.

To pledge allegiance to
Red White and Blue.
Not the old Union but the new
Stars. Things grow

Differently and
Midday sun lasts longer and is
Stronger, here earth's throb is
Close and it's difficult to

Sleep, to dream rain soft
Between wind and cloud where
Rosemary lives at
Christmas. There is no

High Street time when
you only buy leeks,
No salad stuff.
The hour does not settle in

Old women's shopping bags or the
Deep basket of the man going
Along between hedgerows, his
Cloth cap moving like the

Full moon across the landscape.
I have not got used to
Bigger snowdrops, Robins
Without a small paunch

Must weep all of the time.
I raise my hand
With my own voice
Swear, as the

First step into the
New World.

JUDITH ADAMS recently moved to the United States from Great Britain. She became an American citizen in May 1995.

PATRICIA SCHUETZ

Blue Moon

Paul Klee. *Arab Song.*
Gouche on unprimed
burlap, 1932.
Washington, D.C.:
The Phillips Collection.

IT WAS THE SECOND FULL MOON in the calendar month, but it wasn't blue, it was a startling salmon-orange color. I stopped on the sidewalk to marvel at the huge glowing platter, but moved on when I noticed a shadowy figure emerge from between two parked cars across the street. With a lurching stoop-and-stagger, the shape moved in my direction, and I quickened my pace to avoid an encounter.

The nonprofit radio station where I volunteer shares a building with a mental health clinic. One night I had arrived to find a young woman lying curled in the middle of the street, a Walkman on her head, having herself a rollicking tantrum. Tonight I was much later than usual and, except for the lurching stranger, completely alone in the dark. Suddenly alarmed, I gauged the number of steps between me and the door. I began to consider evasive action.

"I beg your pardon, I'm afraid I startled you." The stranger spoke with the lushest, most cultivated voice I had ever heard. I turned to look at him. The moonlight gleamed on a polished walking stick.

I knew this voice. Its owner read the great English romantic poets —Byron, Tennyson, John Donne—for broadcast to a print-impaired audience, Tuesday nights from eleven till one. My own contribution—a weekly news magazine—aired just ahead of his, from ten till eleven. When I first volunteered at the station, I would tune in at home to hear myself on tape; *Nightscape* followed immediately, and often I fell asleep to the voice of the man who called himself "Lawrence."

The remarkable thing about radio is that all of a person's substance comes through (perhaps you might even say one's spirituality), without any hint of the form. The subtlety of his inflection, the range of his mimic ability, told me this was a thoughtful, sensitive man who had lived a full life and learned from it. Sight unseen, any woman would want to know Lawrence. Still, because sighted people always need a picture, my mind had attached to the deep, burly voice, a sort of Lawrence-of-Arabia figure. As I looked at the stick, I adjusted the image of a tall, graceful man to accommodate a serious limp. Curious to see how his face would compare with the Lawrence I had imagined, I said, "Yes, a little. Never mind. Can I hold the door for you?"

From the shadows he answered, "Thank you, no. I think I'll stay and have a cigarette."

"Ah," I said. I could make out nothing but the angled brim of his hat. "Well, I'm on-air in fifteen minutes. I'd better be moving along."

"Cynthia, isn't it?" he asked. "*Time Magazine*?"

"Yes," I said, delighted that he knew me. "I've always pretaped the show, so we've never met. Today they were short an engineer; they asked if I'd come in late and do it live. And you are . . . Lawrence?"

"I am," he said. "I would offer my hand but I'm afraid I'm a little unsteady."

"That's quite all right," I murmured. "Well, wish me luck, Lawrence. I've never done this live."

"Your maiden fight without a net." His phrases were streams of soft, bright bubbles set loose on an evening breeze. "The trick I use is to imagine I'm reading to a single captivated person."

"Thanks. Good advice," I said.

I left him lighting his cigarette in the shadow of a tree and opened the door to the half-lit empty lobby. In the suite occupied by the radio station, I passed the control room and called out a greeting to Lydia, the night engineer. I had learned by now not to exclaim if I found her running the station in the dark—lights or no, it was all the same to her. I walked to the prep room, poured myself coffee, found the new copy of *Time* in my bin, and began to lay out my program.

Minutes later, the monitor in the prep room came on. "You can use the right-hand studio tonight," called Lydia. "The clock in there's broken, so watch the control room. I'll give you all the time cues."

"Right-o." I gathered my coffee, my purse, and my pile of clippings.

"Remember," she said, "you're going live. You don't have to i.d. a tape."

"No i.d.," I repeated. I walked from the prep room to the on-air studio, trying not to think how many ways I could embarrass myself in an hour. It was mortifying to find you had been mispronouncing the name of General Babangida. I had, the past year, been known to hiccup, burp, sneeze and fall asleep at the mike; always Lydia or another engineer had been able to back up the tape and cover the goof. Lawrence was right, a live broadcast was going to be like flying without a net. My pile of clippings was gummy in my anxious grip.

I twisted the microphone arm to suit my height, arranged my copy in front of me, and looked out the studio window. Across the hall Lydia had turned on her light and was holding three fingers in the air; her free hand went on reading meters and clocks and adjusting what needed adjustment. One finger went down; two minutes to go. I turned up the monitor in the room and listened to Barrie in the studio next door. She was reading a letter to the editor from the local Catholic weekly and was wrapping her program up.

Another of Lydia's fingers went down; then Barrie did her "outro" and I heard the harp music that preceded the station i.d., Christina Rossetti coming up on *Nightscape* at eleven. Now it was time for our weeky newsmagazine.

Lawrence, I thought in a rush of fright. I'm only speaking to Lawrence. "Good evening," I breathed toward the microphone. "This is Cynthia, bringing you *Time Magazine* for the week of August twenty-third."

I got through the first half-hour without a disaster: Bosnia, Palestine, Robert Dole. When Lydia's fingers counted down and then signalled the start of my one-minute break, I tried to stand up and fell into the wall—one of my feet had lost circulation from being twisted around a chair leg. I stamped the blood back into it, and stepped into the hall for a change of air.

"Looking good," called Lydia, busy timing the sixty-second spot. "Thirty seconds to air."

I glanced into the left-hand booth and saw the back of a dark-haired man. There was an open book in one outstretched hand, an ebony cane on the table. I imagined he always pre-read his material, marking the breath stops and figuring out where the emphasis should fall. He never stumbled over a phrase that meant something else when you got to the end of it. Probably he had studied drama. Could you act with a limp? I wondered. Me, I had studied accounting and business; my main qualification for this volunteer job was being able to pronounce *laissez faire*. I could never stand to read a news article twice, so my listeners got it rough and ready, first time out of the box.

"Ten seconds to air," called Lydia, and I darted to the mike and thought out my next dozen words. I had chosen a book review for the second half hour, and a piece on the Vatican art exhibit in Denver. I never knew whether or not to include things like this for an audience that was, after all, mostly sightless. It seemed wrong to label any category of news as inappropriate for a large group of people. If a blind person, I reasoned, couldn't hear book reviews, how would he know what to order from the Library of Congress? What about someone whose life had been painting or sculpture, till disease or injury robbed him of his vision? Wouldn't such a person still want to know what the Pope had seen fit to send on an American tour? I wanted to be a conduit, not a censor, and I chose my articles mainly on personal interest and my sense of proportion.

When my wristwatch showed five minutes to eleven, I began glancing out the window for Lydia's cue. Three fingers went up halfway into a piece on urban mass transit systems, and I slowed my speech a little so the article would end when three minutes were up.

"This has been Cynthia for the past hour, bringing you *Time Magazine*. Stay tuned for *Nightscape* coming up next. And, Lawrence, if you're listening . . . thanks. This one was for you."

I took a deep breath and uncurled myself from my chair. Lydia was making a donut with her fingers, then giving me a thumbs-up through the studio window. Where did a blind person learn gestures, I wondered, as I stood up and stretched out the kinks. From the monitor came the little violin theme that introduced my mysterious colleague. The violin faded, and his deep, lovely voice rumbled forth: "Good evening, to all our regular listeners. Welcome, to our guests. This is Lawrence . . . and this is *Nightscape*." A little pause for dramatic effect, and then, "For those of you who drop in every Tuesday for *Time Magazine:* because of the magic of magnetic tape, you are probably unaware that this program is usually pre-recorded early in the evening. Tonight we are having a personnel crisis in our radio control room, and our good friend Cynthia rose to meet it. The past sixty minutes came to you absolutely live and unedited. Here's to you, Cynthia. Well done."

I looked at Lydia, working the dials and setting up the next spot, to see if she had heard all that, but she gave no indication. I went into the corridor and looked through the window at Lawrence. He hadn't changed his position; I could still see only his hand and the back of his head. From the soundproof booth I could hear the thin echo of the full rolling cadences coming from Lydia's monitor: "Remember me when I am gone away . . . "

"Lydia," I said, when Lydia had a minute to listen to me. "Does Lawrence ever tape his show, or does he always read it live?"

Lydia's face turned toward me, listing slightly side to side as if her skin were radar searching out an object. "Always live. He seems to prefer it that way."

"Because the studio's empty at that hour?"

"I suppose."

"How long has he been doing this?"

"A little longer than you have, I guess. Maybe a year and a half." Lydia was giving away exactly nothing.

"You know anything about him?" I asked.

"Well, he had fancy French pastry sent in for us on his birthday."

"I mean about his personal life."

"Not really. Do you see a tape that says 'Penguins Hockey' on it? Somebody made a real mess in here—I can't find any of my stuff."

I found her the tape.

"So . . . ," I began again, trying to sound offhand. "You think it went okay tonight? Reading live, I mean?"

"I think it went great."

"So . . . what would the program manager think if I went live every week? Save the trouble of taping."

Lydia had her back to me now, as she mounted her hockey tape. "Let it alone, okay?" she said. "I think he needs his space."

Embarrassed that she had so quickly seen though me, I took her advice and abandoned the idea of stalking the mysterious Lawrence. I went home, turned on the television set to the cable channel that carried the radio feed, undressed for the night, slipped into bed, and let Lawrence's silky, urbane baritone carry me off.

I thought a great deal about Lawrence that week. I concluded that whatever had injured his leg had spoiled other things, and that Lawrence was seeking to avoid the stares of the curious or the shocked. Well, I thought, okay, if that's what he wants. But I couldn't seem to follow Lydia's advice and let it alone. I needed to hear him speak to me again.

Next Tuesday the station had its full complement of studio engineers. I went in after work and readied my usual program, but for my final piece I wanted something special. I went back through a file of clippings and found what I wanted: a retrospective on the Restoration poets. That ought to get his attention, I thought. If his studio monitor's on, he can hardly miss it.

I made my tape, and ended with the retrospective on Milton and Pope. At the end I paused, and then I said, "If you're listening, Lawrence—that one was for you."

I signed off, cleared out my booth, labeled the tape for the engineer and went home. From bed I listened patiently to myself as I read about Bosnia, Somalia, and the Dodgers. Finally my book-piece —I read it nicely, I thought—and then I heard my electronic clone burble, "If you're listening, Lawrence . . ."

I twisted my hair impatiently as I waited through the station i.d. Then he was there, alive and in person, saying, "Yes, I was assuredly listening, Cynthia. Thank you. For those of you in radioland who are following this little drama, Cynthia is the lady with the elegant pronunciation whose program airs just before mine. She pretapes, and I am here live, so I fear we are doomed to remain as we are, two ships passing silently in the night. My name is Lawrence . . . and this is *Nightscape*."

I listened to him, curled up in my bed, for almost the entire two hours. It was late, and toward the end I started to doze. At last I heard Lawrence—or dreamed I did—whisper in a voice full of honey and musk, "Good night, Cynthia. Sweet dreams."

I had wonderful dreams full of Lawrence that night—Lawrence without a body or a face. I woke up to the morning news and the song of a robin outside, and in the clear light of day, I wondered if Lawrence had really wished me goodnight.

The following Tuesday the station manager waylaid me in the prep room and removed any doubt. He was holding a handful of mail as he said, with a grin, "Do you mind if I ask what's going on between you and Mr. Alejandro?"

"Mr. . . . ." The name meant nothing to me.

"Lawrence, Mr. Nightscape. To judge from the fan mail, I missed something extraordinary last week."

"Fan mail," I echoed.

"Some of our listeners think you and he should combine your shows into one."

I laughed at that. "Could we work economic projections into a romantic literary format?"

"As a station manager," he said, "I can't recommend it. One guy wants Lawrence to call you up on the air, and a lady named Mrs. Ida Shemansky says she'll cook if you both have dinner with her."

I laughed again, but it wasn't so funny. Instead I was a little bit startled to realize the thirst for romance out there in radioland. "It sounds as if Lawrence and I have stumbled into the middle of a lot of people's fantasies. What do you know about him?" I asked, still trying hard to anchor Lawrence to something in the real world. "Is he an actor?"

"Close. He was a broadcast journalist, till his accident made a career in front of a camera a little unlikely. TV's loss is radio's gain— he's got a sensational voice."

"Well," I said, "I don't know if anything will ever come of this. I'd love to meet him, but in social relationships I guess I'm a risk-averse person. Lawrence is just going to have to make the next move."

That night as as I came to the end of my hour and moved into my outro, I took a deep breath and leaned into my mike. "Good night, take care, I'll be back next week. And Lawrence . . . if you have a phone book, I'm usually home Wednesday nights."

Lawrence began his own broadcast on a note of ironic drama: "And so it continues, dear listener, the unfolding romance of Cynthia and Lawrence. Can a good pronouncer of foreign names, and the voice of your midnight fantasies, find happiness across the radio waves? Stay tuned. And now . . . _Nightscape_."

Lawrence actually called me the following evening. When the phone rang in my little apartment, I realized I had been listening for it and lifted the receiver with an eager, unsteady hand.

"Hello." I held my breath, preparing myself for likely disappointment. It was probably my mother. Probably the office.

"Cynthia. Good evening." It was he, and I began to breathe again.

"Lawrence. How lovely. Let me just turn the radio down."

We talked for two hours. About books, about people. We talked in a tentative, cautiously self-revelatory way, handing over discrete little bits of ourselves, then bigger bits. We talked about families, careers, schools, assembling the bits into coherent pictures, like a thousand-piece jigsaw puzzle that made a rose garden. He mentioned his accident only in passing—said he'd used half the insurance money to endow a little theater and with the income from the other half he kept an apartment, a dog, a cook, a car, and a driver.

At the end of two hours, having established enough common interest to carry us this far, it was clear to me an invitation was in order. "Lawrence," I said, "would you think I was pushing if I invited you over for dinner? That way we could go on talking without getting cauliflower ears."

There followed a very, very long silence, during which I could hear the quiet, regular breathing at the end of the line.

At last he said, in a thoughtful, dignified way, "Cynthia, the radio and the telephone are astonishing inventions. Astonishing in their ability to mediate reality and intercept one of its dimensions."

"I understand what you're saying," I said. "I think it's not a problem."

There was another long and painful silence. Then he said, "Do you remember the story of Eros and Psyche?"

Yes, I remembered. Eros, the virile young god, fell in love with a girl. He was a smart enough god to appreciate the difference in their circumstances, and he also wanted to be loved for himself. Thus, he arranged to visit Psyche at night. He came to her without a lamp, and told her if she loved him she would never try to see him.

So, I thought. Lydia said it—Lawrence needs his space. I mustn't try to see him. I could have wept with disappointment.

Then Lawrence said, "There's a new play on that theme opening at my theater on Friday. If you'd like, I'll send my driver for you."

Nearly speechless, I said yes, I'd like it very much. Yes, at half past seven. See you Friday.

Thursday dragged, and Friday must have stopped dead in its tracks a dozen times. I had long since prepared myself for anything—scars, burns, boils, missing features, missing bones. Somehow I couldn't interest myself in all that now—in my mind I was already making love to Lawrence in his mind.

From my front window I watched the sleek black Cutlass with smoked windows drive up to my building.

"Miss Franklin?" asked the driver as I came out onto the sidewalk. I nodded, and he opened the door of the car. I peered inside. The car was empty.

"Mr. Alejandro?" I asked the driver, startled.

"Mr. Alejandro's been held up. He'll meet you at the theater."

The theater was *very* little—the basement of a pharmacy, with exactly sixty-two seats arranged in two tiers around the stage. I counted the seats as I waited for Lawrence, and by ones and twos I watched them fill with normal-looking people. The seats on either side of mine were taken up by women, and when the lights went out, every seat but one was filled. That one seat was right across the little stage from mine, and it was empty as a missing tooth when the actors came onstage.

Eros and Psyche, as I had been promised. The god of love and the nitwitted beauty. She loved, she lusted, she worshiped him, sight unseen. But being an essentially visual person, Psyche couldn't let it alone. She had to have the picture.

Damn it, Lawrence, I thought to myself, convinced by then that he had lost his nerve and stood me up. We can't help the fact that we're sighted human beings. I think, for the sake of a kind of friendship that comes along once in a blue moon, we ought to make an effort to neutralize the visual dimension.

I watched the play in simmering frustration. It was an elegant, sensual little production, acted well enough to let you feel the heat between the principals. I wanted Lawrence. At last a little commotion distracted me from the stage. The usher was showing a late-arrival to the seat across from me. I knew that limping walk, and that silver-headed stick. I felt my heart stop.

I understood then what he'd had in mind. This was Lawrence's way of sparing us both an embarrassing encounter. I could, if I wanted, get up and leave, and pretend with perfect plausibility I'd never seen him. In which he could conspire by saying he'd been held up and hadn't made it after all, so sorry. Lawrence was a gentleman, all right.

He had come in wearing his hat, brim tilted low to hide his face. I watched him scan my row of seats, and slowly take the hat off.

I smiled. He smiled, and I studied him.

Well, yes, I would have to say his features were distracting—nose off-center, mouth a little crooked, and even in the stage light I could see there was some scarring. For a man who had been handsome, I suppose it was a shock.

As for me, though, I could feel my insides doing cartwheels—Lawrence was sitting forty feet away and smiling at me. I made a finger-donut, Lydia-style, and winked at him. See you after the show, I mouthed, and Lawrence signaled back and winked at me.

PATRICIA SCHUETZ, a systems programmer for the Mellon Bank in Pittsburgh, has been a writer for twenty-five years. Her short stories have appeared in university publications and the small press. Mrs. Schuetz is presently working on three novels, a sort of once-in-a-blue-moon occupation.

CAROL LEM

Sea of Spring

But it was she and not the sea we heard.
—WALLACE STEVENS

I raise the black lid
of my shakuhachi case,
stare at two bamboo flutes
quiet as lovers. I pick the longer one
up, stroke the five holes,
breathe into the slender tube, as if
to say I'm here, I'm ready.

Fingers in place, I blow low D
like OM with the lips
caressing the sound as it reaches
down to the belly, circles darkness,
rises, my head gently shaking.
Sound dips in and out, as I climb the scale
testing each pitch to high C
where the air is clear.
I linger on the mountain peak
holding the note without falling
until it wavers and disappears
into the sound of one hand.

I spread the music on the floor,
Haru no Umi, sit back on my heels,
and enter the sea, imaging spring
above this busy boulevard.
A wave foams around my legs,
pauses by a gathering of stones.

I listen to blackbirds peck across
rooftops before riding the crest
of another wave.

It is the sea, not me
playing this tune.
The sea, not me
filling my small room
with jasmine blossoms.

Born in Los Angeles, CAROL LEM teaches creative writing and literature at East Los Angeles College. Her poems have been published in *Blue Mesa, Hawaii Pacific Review, The Illinois Review, The Lucid Stone, The Seattle Review,* and many other publications.

PART II

The Voyage Out, Alone

With hopes that one day my head would clear, for the next two years each evening I stood on the roof of my tiny adobe house in San Miguel de Allende, facing northeast to Leda and Wendy and Peter, and wept. On my fiftieth birthday Leda sent me a beautiful shawl from her loom with a note that read, "Does September happen in Mexico too?"

ONCE FOUND, AN OPENING MUST BE STEPPED THROUGH OR LOST. Swedenborg called this step *Turning Around* and illustrates it by God's dividing the light from the darkness in Creation. It requires turning back from cherished purposes, turning away from familiar ways, turning against principles—and sometimes friends—we have relied on.

It is a lonely turn, often threatening, always without guarantee of success or even safety. Its unknown consequences may lend desirability to what is familiar and make experience appear as a better guide than hope. But the alternative to turning around is staying stuck at the beginning, before change, possibility, or growth. Not turning toward the future means remaining in the present we were waiting to get out of, a present that is tarnished forever by our new awareness that something better calls us from beyond the unknown.

The voyage out, alone, gets us somewhere, even if not where we intended, as in "This Color Is My Skin." It leaves us richer, even when it takes from us the prize we sought, as in "Precious Jade." Whether we are turning away from tradition, as in "Pop's Church," familiar behavior, as in "A Blue-Ridge Christmas," what preachers call sin, or a dead-end job or life style, turning around is the only way from here to there. The only route from one order to a better one runs through the messy middle of disorder and along the middle ground defined by Tony Mitton.

ABIGAIL CALKINS

This Color Is My Skin

Abigail Calkins joined the Peace Corps in 1987 in search of "doing good." During her first month in Cameroon she learned it was harder than it sounded.

I COULD WALK IN ANY DIRECTION, I am free to the evening, I have no constraints. Or, at least, not many. The road to the other American's house is the one I take because it is what I know and all the rest is a bit scary. Night has already fallen and fallen hard—a pitch black because there are no street lamps and few house lights, and that, along with my miserable night vision, makes me stumble in and out of puddles. At least I'm somewhat less conspicuous in this darkness, yet the children's giggles as I pass say I am fluorescent to them, like a neon sign flashing WHITE WHITE WHITE, compelling me to walk quickly and greet only those who greet me. I remember listening to *Strangers in the Night* from my great aunt's wooden music box in Boston. I feel like more than just a stranger here. Something akin to an alien, I smile wryly to myself.

I walk past the women merchants, seated in a row with their soft lanterns glowing, displaying tonight's selection of spicy fish heads neatly arranged next to chewy licorice-like cassava sticks. The Small Store behind them sells canned sardines and stale french bread. Water trickles from a community pump between these two markets. Further up the road, there is an ancient truck, abandoned and growing green and wild like a huge, surreal planter. Just after that, my Cameroonian co-worker's house sits on the left. She is standing outside under a fluorescent light, braiding her sister's hair. This woman is my first real connection to the local population that goes slightly beyond superficiality. She is my designated godmother, the woman who knows how to be with whites because she has been with so many already and that's no joke either: there is status to these things. I plan on slinking by unnoticed, but in a small town where every move has a witness, this plan fails. I am spotted by my coworker and beckoned.

I go to her and we shake hands. She still has a hard time with my name—it is too Anglo-Saxon. She invites me into her house, which doubles as a bar, sometimes as a restaurant. The woman is incredible—has a full-time job with the government in Community Development, and then sells beer at home to supplement her weak salary so she can feed her three kids plus her sister plus her sister's kids plus her mother plus any other passing needy soul. A real African woman and family. Except for the fact that she is divorced. And she is liberated, independent, in a way different from the rest. Whether this is the effect of working for years beside American women is unknown. A possiblity.

I figure, what the hell, why not go in, a way to kill time, to mingle, get to know the town a little better, not always spend my evenings enveloped in the security of my fellow American. Poking my head

John Biggars.
Fishing Village.
Conté crayon, 40 × 37 inches, 1962.
Hampton, Virginia: Hampton University Museum.

through the curtained door, I behold the brightly lit room with several men sitting in oversized furniture around a coffee table, bottles of beer half empty, empty, and full, set in a jumble before them. They are in the midst of an animated discussion. On what? Sports? Moment of hesitation: I have the sense of stepping before a conveyor belt that appears to have no appropriate place for me. But it is too late. My head is already through the door.

"Miss, come in! What are you afraid of? Drink a beer with us, we're not going to eat you."

What am I afraid of? I enter and shake each person's hand as introductions are made. Some I have already met before, but sorting faces and titles out has been confusing. Here is the town's Commissioner of Police, the Director of the Bank, the Discipline Master of the Secondary School, and the Company Commander of the Military. A bureaucrat's bar with an impressive crew. And I am the New Volunteer, come to replace the Old.

They make room for me. I have a throne-like easy chair all to my small self. It's meant to be comfortable, luxurious in its ampleness, but the way the head cushion jets out makes me feel awkward, as if I were a chicken stuck in a pecking position. A large beer materializes before me. I pour. We toast to our health and I set myself to drinking it methodically as the conversation wanders on without me. My thoughts follow a different frequency here, like a shortwave radio searching a signal from afar. It is a game I play sometimes, more often now, borrowing clips from the past, reruns of conversations with friends and ex-lovers, images of walking on the beach, movies, ice cream, late night TV, Mexican food, superhighways, snow and all things which now seem fabricated, untrue, next to what I have before me.

"Miss, how do you find the town?"

Someone must have noticed my isolation. "Fine. Very fine," I glance up, still in a trance, halfway in the United States, halfway out. "The people are very friendly."

"You have been here for how long now?"

"One month."

"And how long will you be here with us?"

"Two years," I say, somewhat in disbelief. *Two years?* An extraordinary figure to be rattling off my tongue like that.

"What do you do?"

My first month. What do I do?

I get on my moto, my co-worker mounts behind me and we go out together and save the world. No, that's not exactly it. I get on my moto, my co-worker mounts behind me, we conquer the roads and do what we can with the women's groups. I go to the office and wait for my new boss to arrive, the old one having been fired for extorting goods, poor management. I get on my moto, my co-worker mounts behind me, it rains, we turn around and slip-slide all the way back home. I go to the office and look through old files, notes from training. I get on my moto, my co-worker mounts behind me and we argue about how many times (if at all) we will stop to shop for bushmeat. I go to the office, I read a book, sometimes technical, sometimes fiction. I get on my moto, my co-worker refuses to mount behind me. I go to the office. I get on my moto.

"I work in Community Development," I hear myself saying, sipping my beer.

"She's my co-worker," my co-worker points out as she clears some bottles from the table.

"We work with women's groups. Nutrition. Demonstrations. Community farms . . ." I add.

"I see. And what nationality are you?"

This is how the questions progress, how they have progressed ever since I first arrived in the town. I provide the crowd with my general credentials: nationality, state, age, family members (no, I don't have any brothers) . . . We talk in cordial tones, and the beer sinks low in the glasses, so someone orders another round, and the tone becomes more familiar, the laughter a bit more raucous, the gestures more pronounced. Some ask questions about American politics and I answer what I can. They answer the rest. Strange, almost eerie, how they know more facts about the States than many Americans. And when they ask me what Americans know about Cameroon, I'm embarrassed to say how little.

"Miss, you must stay in this country forever. Never go back to your country. Become a Cameroonian," invites the Discipline Master.

I think about my family and friends at home, about writing them and saying that I've decided to stay here forever. The thought drains me. Some days, like today, two years seems an eternity. I scold myself. That's not the right attitude to have. Why can't I be more like Isak Dinesen, who thought benevolently even when her plantation was ruined, her lover killed and she was forced involuntarily out of Africa?

"You must marry a black man and have black babies and live here forever," says the Director of the Bank.

I smile wearily. I hear this all the time. I was hoping we wouldn't land on this subject. What am I supposed to say?

"I want a white woman," the Company Commander announces, his manner more aggressive, testing, than the others. "You must marry me and have my babies and I'll give you some land where you will cultivate groundnuts and your hands will have callouses from the hoe . . ."

People are laughing, looking at me, waiting for my comeback. A comeback is expected. After all, I am the one white woman in the room, and white women is what this conversation is about. Impossible to have a neutral presence with skin that blares. There is always some sort of reaction or association, like those who treat me like a movie star, a queen, a witch, a wench, a joke, a ghost, a dollar sign. Or the people who make references to the Good Lord and Our Savior and then ask me if I am with the Catholic Mission; the very same people who call me "Sister" and sort of bow in reverence, as if I could bless them with a greeting, as if my whiteness equaled piousness.

I throw a glance for help at my co-worker, but she is busy serving more beer, and her silence tells me that I am expected to defend myself. I'm supposed to find this amusing—everyone else seems to—but I am inclined to seriousness. I can't laugh because I don't think it's funny.

"I say," says the Commander petulantly, "I want a white woman."

"I see," I reply uncomfortably, thinking, if it's the color white you're after, why don't you just buy a bucket of paint and . . . I keep my glass to my lips as a sort of shield.

"I will make you my third wife," he persists.

"In the United States," I retort, feeling almost vindictive, "polygamy is illegal." I'm losing my patience. So is the Commander. I feel the beer. So must we all.

"Whites can't stand polygamy," reports the Discipline Master.

"Why?" asks the Director of the Bank, annoyed.

"White women are too jealous. They go crazy," he says.

"That's not it," I start to protest.

"Man cannot be expected to eat plantains everyday. How can you expect him to stay with just one woman?" queries the Director.

"You will accustom yourself to polygamy with me," the Commander orders.

"I have a boyfriend already," I say finally, glaring at them, feeling a wave of self-contempt for coming to that now frequently used excuse, hating them for forcing me to resort to it, disliking above all the implication that "I'm not up for grabs, I already have an owner," but I use it out of desperation, wanting to be left alone, not knowing how to deal with this coffee-table harassment. I would tell them all to go to hell if we were in the States.

"Yes, but a boyfriend is not a husband! Surely it doesn't infringe on us getting to 'know' each other better!"

"Where is this 'boyfriend' anyhow?"

"You must leave him for me."

"Is his skin this color?" asks the Director, pointing to his own skin, "Or this color?" pointing to mine.

"His skin is this color," I say, pointing to the blue tablecloth. No, that's a lie — I don't say that, but I should. All my best lines, the light, humorous kind, come to me later at night as I'm lying alone in bed. Instead, I make some philosophical comment about color not needing to matter and then my co-worker speaks out all of a sudden and tells them he is white, and everyone looks at me with contempt. I feel betrayed and alone.

"You must give your heart to a Cameroonian man before you can really understand Cameroonian culture," suggests the Discipline Master.

The Bank Director snorts, "You Americans are so racist. You come to Africa and out of all of the black people there are to choose from, you pick another white!"

"If I were racist," I say desperately, "I wouldn't be here in the first place."

"That's untrue," says the Director firmly. "You whites come here to pity the blacks. We don't need your pity. Your pity is in itself racist."

Annoyed, I blurt out, "Oh, you Cameroonian men!" hoping to stop the conversation point blank, but I see by the reaction in the crowd that offense has been taken, and all this does is change the pace of the discussion.

"What do you mean 'Cameroonian' men?" the Commissioner, silent until now, asks.

I want to put this evening out of its misery but I don't know how. I don't like being the white spokesperson. I'm failing at it miserably. I'm tired. Tired, why? All I have done today is sleep.

I suppose I could leave, but I feel mysteriously glued to my chair by the forces of local custom—my beer isn't finished yet. And just at that moment, the Commander orders yet a new round. I look at the quart bottle in front of me with the disbelief of someone asked to scale the Washington Monument with no hands, wincing as my co-worker opens it before I can stop her. Not the others though. They heartily down their last beer, eager to attack the latest arrival, the adrenalin of the debate intensifying their thirst.

"That's the thing," begins the Commander, who has now moved up in his chair, having watched the entire debate at play and apparently coming to some sort of conclusion. "You whites come over here trying to help us, judging us an inferior culture. Undeveloped. You call us barbaric, but if you go to Europe, all the women are parading nude on the beaches. Who, I ask you, is barbaric? You call us filthy because our skin is black, but you whites go for days without bathing, as you hitchhike across this continent. Who is filthier? You come to this country with your cameras and take pictures of those of us who are barefoot, those of us who are sick or starving, and then you take these pictures back to your land of whites and you say: 'This is poverty in Africa! Aren't the blacks pathetic!'"

How did we get here? I have three-fourths of this last bottle of beer to go. If it were empty, I could leave. It is my hourglass of sorts. Why do they make beer bottles so big in this damn country?

"Excuse me," I say, frustrated, "you are making generalizations. Not all whites are alike . . ."

To which his stormy reply comes, "Excuse me, but you are white. Period. I will tell you something, my dear. There are three races of people in the world: Black, on whom all the shit of mankind has been placed. Yellow, who have taken their fair share. And white, who have dished it all out to everyone."

I am silent. The air is charged enough with electric accusations and I already feel the unpleasant warning signal at the base of my throat—a volcano of tears about to erupt, bubbling from down inside. Oh crap, just whatever you do, don't cry.

I pick up my glass, forcing what is left in it down, and start to put on my jeans jacket. The beer is hard to swallow—it has to wrestle with my clenched throat. Out of this frantic attempt to escape, I hear the Commissioner's fatherly command: "Where are you going? You are going to stay here and finish this conversation."

"Some day," the Director shakes his finger at me, "the blacks are going to come to America and make the whites slaves just like you did to us!" General approval from the crowd. My co-worker is watching from behind the Discipline Master's chair.

That's it. I bend my head and tears begin to spill down into my lap. There is too much not to cry. Why are they being so mean? And what can I say to heal the wound, to soothe the children of those wronged and wronged themselves by an arbitrary factor of color and culture? An image dislodges itself from my memory just at this moment: that of our small group of college students vehemently protesting apartheid on our college campus, our fists held defiantly up in the air. From here, we look like ants and I suddenly feel foolish. I want to say something, anything, damn it.

But all I do is cry.

And they sit there and watch me cry and they are surprised, as if this weren't the logical conclusion to such a debate.

"What's this? She's crying?"

"My daughter, why are you crying?"

"Oh, come now, don't cry. We were only joking."

"Just jokes, my dear, you mustn't take things so seriously."

"You can't be so sensitive. One cannot be sensitive in Africa!"

"To see a white person cry . . . supposedly the strongest people in the world! And an American at that! We can't have this!"

I do my best to pull myself together, stand up, still sniffling, and shake everyone's hand. I say, "I really must go, I don't feel well." No one protests this time.

My co-worker follows me outside, where the fluorescent light from her house shines on us both. She takes my hands in hers and faces me. She asks me what is wrong and I look into her eyes and see pain? . . . or is it disappointment? Have I somehow failed her? I tell her I cannot explain why I am so sad, knowing that an explanation will just provoke more crying. She sighs, observing my tear-stained face and asks quietly:

"My friend, is your heart that weak?"

I WALK HOME AND TAKE A COLD SHOWER. I ignore the hot water heater which I disconnected because they told me that it would double my electric bills, and I can't afford that on this salary. The shower is very brief. Shivering, I dry off with my mildewed towel which I make note to wash tomorrow if I find the energy. I pick up my toothbrush and examine it suspiciously, thinking of the other toothbrush I just threw away after discovering a king-sized cockroach sucking on it one surprise 3 a.m. visit to the bathroom.

In my bedroom, I take my small hand mirror and run a critical inspection from feet to knees to thighs to stomach breasts neck chin mouth nose, stopping when I make contact with my eyes. I am so pale, as if someone bleached me. Two years to go.

ABIGAIL CALKINS was a community-development Peace Corps volunteer in Cameroon, Central Africa, from 1987 to 1990. She currently lives and works in Ciudad Juarez, Mexico, as Resident Advisor for the Cooperative Housing Foundation, an international nonprofit organization that specializes in affordable shelter solutions for low-income people.

CORRINE DE WINTER

Cocoon

For two years
The cancer worked to overwhelm you,
A heavy-handed stranger
Putting down roots.
For two years you pushed
Through suffering,
A pilgrim in pain's wilderness.

And then it happened,
Perhaps just as you'd imagined
A hundred times over.
In the after hours
Of a sharp July evening
You were lifted
From the bleached hospital sheets
Which made you paler by the hour,
Slipped from the tubes,
The cold machines,
From the backlash of radiation
That made cinders of your heart.

Removed from a blind hunger,
From the cessation of dreams
You became the dream, the dreamer,
The spirit that quivers
In all living things.

A Pushcart Prize Nominee, CORRINE DE WINTER is the author of six collections of poetry and prose. Her work has appeared in over 400 literary journals and magazines, including *Chrysalis, Touchstone, The Alembic, The Other Side,* and *Conscience.*

TONY MITTON

Order and Disorder

The Middle Ground

WHAT MAKES A GOOD LIFE? Moral theory has a habit of falling apart when confronted with the warm humanity of an actual life. For five years I lived in close proximity to a friend and teacher whose auto-biography has just been posthumously published.[1] To encounter Peter Caddy was to enter a Tolkien-like landscape where legends sprang to life and modern-day materialist outlooks were turned on their head. Then was he mentally deranged or a fraud? The simple honesty of his approach made one think otherwise. He seemed more real than life. To read his book is like riding a steeplechase packed with fences, jumps, and hazards. One event succeeds another at breakneck pace.

Peter was born into an unremarkable and rather narrow English middle-class family. He remarks that he "inherited characteristics from both parents: order and stamina from my father, disorder and a wish to care for people from Mother."[2] The two themes, order and disorder, play point and counterpoint throughout his life. It is to Peter's credit that he evolved a central core around which they wove. This was not a core of ego such as often afflicts powerful men, but a quest for truth, a love of God and a desire to serve. His father was a strict Methodist, but, suffering from chronic pain, sought help from a medium. Attending some of the sessions, the young Peter sensed that something real was happening and, thus introduced to the realm of the unseen, he never looked back.

He finished high school, an indifferent scholar but a good ath-lete, and joined Lyons, Britain's largest catering firm, as a management trainee. Then he married his first wife, Nora. Nora's brother-in-law introduced them both to a secret order of Rosicrucians, with whom Peter embarked on a course of initiation along the path of light, truth, and reason. Distributed through his autobiography are excerpts from their teachings which served him throughout life. Their thrust is to enhance awareness of the God Within: at the spiritual level by invoking divine love and truth; at the soul level, by emphasizing one's own power and intelligence derived from the divine; and at the human level by loving where you are, what you do, and whom you are with, being accountable, and seeing the good in everything.

Soon, World War II broke out, and Peter was commissioned into the catering branch of the Royal Air Force. As a junior officer assigned to introduce centralized messing to his Wing, he used his athleticism to make himself recreational officer, a post influential with superiors and subordinates alike. From this unconventional power-base on the sports field, he was able to persuade the twenty-six independent and very competitive messes to adopt centralized control of personnel, procurement, and a system of master menus. This became the model for the air force. Posted to India, he used leave periods to lead treks into the Himalayas, some taking him to India's more inaccessible and holy places. In January 1945, he was promoted to be Command Catering Officer for the Burma front where the allied armies were fighting the Japanese. After the war was over, he led two expeditions deep into Tibet. His climbs in India seem inspired by a simple love of mountaineering, but his expeditions into Tibet appear to be driven by a spiritual need, as if he wished to absorb the soul of Buddhism from its very heart.

Returning to Britain after the war, Peter was posted to the Air Ministry in London. Nora, however, preferred to live near the Rosicrucian headquarters, one hundred and fifty miles away. Nora's life revolved around her mother and their son, and Peter felt like an intruder. Taking the train to travel down one weekend, he encountered Sheena Govan. So far, order had ruled in Peter's life. Now, disorder entered. Sheena was a "psychic," receiving spiritual guidance during meditations, and was convinced that our planet could be transformed through love. She felt her mission was to help people go through an initiatory experience of self-realization, which she called the birth of the Christ within. Usually, this birth involved their renouncing some treasured trait that was obstructing their growth.

Completely in love, Peter was ready to accept Sheena as his lover and teacher. He divorced Nora and began a wild ride along a new and different path of spiritual initiation, one leading through love, obedience, suffering, sacrifice, and humiliation. From the Rosicrucians and from Buddhism, Peter had acquired a belief in reincarnation, and he now committed himself to fulfilling all his karma in this one lifetime, and so separate himself from the cycle of birth and death.[3] He called this, "climbing his Mountain." He relates how his resolve saddened Sheena, who foresaw the additional suffering it must bring, but he felt himself prepared to accept whatever God sent him. He had already been rejected by his family and the Rosicrucians. Now, Sheena allowed herself to be convinced by a mutual friend and spiritual adept that she must bear that person's child, who was to be the New Messiah. The child was never carried to term. Though horrified, Peter forgave the man and married Sheena. At her insistence however, they later separated and divorced, though Sheena remained his teacher.

In the Middle East, traveling on duty for the Royal Air Force, Peter met Eileen, wife of a senior officer. At first he was not attracted, seeing her as a kind and motherly person, but suddenly his intuition took over and he felt his soul drawn to her in an extraordinary way. He made Eileen his third wife, and, incredibly, Sheena undertook Eileen's spiritual training too. All during this time, Peter had been steadily climbing the career ladder in the Royal Air Force. He became the first catering officer ever to enter RAF Staff College, where outstanding officers are trained for high command. Now, Sheena said that she had received guidance that he must resign from the service!

Why did Peter obey? Mainly because his own powerful intuition told him she was right. This intuition was his greatest strength, a guide at all the major turning points of his life, and many lesser ones. It was, however, neither infallible nor under his control, often failing to manifest when he thought he most needed it, but surfacing instead at inconvenient moments to prompt actions seemingly devoid of common sense, but which in hindsight proved mostly correct. Peter had been led to expect that his Rosicrucian initiation would give him powers to see and hear in the spiritual worlds, but this had not occurred. To compensate, he was rather dependent on the guidance of psychics, such as that which Sheena was now imparting. Moreover, the renunciation of career, the ultimate challenge for many men, coincided with the ideal of sacrifice and humiliation demanded by her model of initiation.

Now began a period of unemployment and odd jobs. Peter was sure that he and Eileen were destined to fulfill an important part of God's plan together, but Sheena would have none of this, maintaining that they were putting each other before God. Obediently, they separated and suffered apart, but finally broke with Sheena. Eventually, Peter became manager of Cluny Hill, a large hotel in

Forres, in northern Scotland. Here, he applied the lessons learned from the Rosicrucians, Sheena, and RAF Staff College, but also began to rely on Eileen who was receiving guidance from an inner voice. With her help, he raised the hotel's rating from three to four stars. For this, he got no thanks from the general manager who only wanted a stopping place for the company's bus tours. But for Peter, only perfection was good enough. He told the story of how he was continually indenting for silver sauce-boats appropriate to the stylish dining-room. Eventually, one dozen sauce-boats were delivered. Joyfully, Peter went to unpack them. To his horror, he found they were of the cheapest crockery variety. Deliberately, one by one, he smashed them on the kitchen floor in front of the van driver, whom he knew to be the general manager's spy.

He made a success of Cluny Hill and, very much against his will, was transferred to upgrade a hotel in southern Scotland that was doing badly. Here his best efforts failed; he was fired and thrust on welfare, now with responsibility for his wife Eileen and the three children who had been born to them. Settling on a caravan site at Findhorn, not far from Cluny Hill, Peter started a garden out of necessity to supplement their diet. Now he began to see justification for his faith that Eileen and he together were to play a part in God's Plan. When Dorothy Maclean, their former secretary at Cluny Hill, came to join them, she began to receive communications from an order of angelic beings who are responsible for the specific species of plants. Both angels and humans were surprised at the encounter, but joyfully eager to experiment with collaboration. For a time the garden produced vegetables of astonishing size and succulence and attracted attention from the far corners of Britain (though chiefly from the locals who came regularly to buy the surplus).[4]

Eventually, Eileen received guidance that Findhorn must begin to grow people instead of plants. The gardens remain a place of power and beauty, but have been outpaced by the community which has grown up around them. Founded on principles of cooperation and planetary service, it seeks to develop a group consciousness of God. Eileen no longer gives out her guidance and there is no dogma and no guru. Rather, individuals look within to find their own guidance. 'Unity in Diversity' and 'Work is Love Made Manifest' are two of the community's watchwords.

Peter gradually relinquished leadership of the Findhorn Community. He divorced Eileen and began a period of wandering and personal growth, marrying again and entering on one other significant relationship before settling with Renata, his fifth wife, in southern Germany. Until his death at the age of 77, they remained actively engaged in the spiritual redemption of the planet, lecturing, joining pilgrimages, making an expedition to the Amazon rain forest, and helping peace efforts in Bosnia.

Peter Caddy lived an extraordinary life, but was it good? One may measure a life by the standards of the person who lives it, by the world's standards, and by its outcomes. Peter certainly strove to live his life according to the values he cherished, so, by his own standards, it was good. The world judges differently and has two sets of standards, religious and secular.

Peter was principally influenced by Christianity, albeit in the Rosicrucian sense, which sees the Christ figure in every religion. Because they have also sought the truth, agnostics and atheists nourish this concept in their hearts too. The Church fathers adopted the four Platonic virtues, wisdom with prudence, courage with fortitude, justice with righteousness, and temperance. They added the Pauline virtues of faith, hope, and love, and later, patience and humility. Peter took the virtue of wisdom with prudence to a new dimension, discarding prudence in favor of intuition. According to people who knew him, toward the end of his life he began to embody wisdom and love together. These two qualities belong together, as instanced by the Greek Church which ascribes them to St. Sophia. Of the other virtues, Peter personified courage and fortitude. On one of his Tibetan expeditions, he and a companion had to trek nearly 60 miles in one stretch, returning at night through a blizzard and climbing three times to over 14,000 feet, to rescue some members of the party who had lagged behind. The virtue of justice with righteousness was important to him, for at certain times in his life he had significant power. He was a strict disciplinarian, but first made sure that his staff were willing to embrace his ideals and methods. And he was temperate, except in his loves.

One would expect Peter, as a disciple of Christ, to exemplify the Pauline virtues of faith, hope, and charity. Certainly, one of Peter's outstanding characteristics was his faith. It was a rock-like knowing which led him unwavering through tests and experiences which shook even this reader of his biography, who thought he knew him. He used faith to co-create, making it "the evidence of things unseen."[5] Faith meant holding a vision and then releasing it in absolute trust that it would come to pass. And because he was no layabout, he would then take whatever practical action was possible. Very often, the method worked. "The universe responds to action" was one of his favorite sayings. Love was his too, but in a different meaning than that conventionally attached. He gave his love to God and that had consequences, demanding discipline, order, responsibility and perfection, but he did not see these as obligations and imposed, but as joyful and fulfilling. But I remember his speaking rather disparagingly of hope, which he saw as containing an element of doubt which could undermine faith.

Patience he learned with the Rosicrucians, and humility Sheena taught him. He needed that lesson. He had early acquired that independence of spirit which is a mark of greatness but can swell into arrogance and pride. In his book, he tells the story of how in India, his commanding officer, a Group Captain, insisted on joining one of his mountaineering parties. Because mountain climbing involves an element of danger and his crew must be a team, Peter told him, "Well, sir, you know you'll have to take your orders from me, and just be one of the boys, having to peel potatoes and so on." The Group Captain, an officer with thirty-five years service and 10,000 men under his command, agreed. There was about Peter a certain harmlessness and simplicity. It found expression not only in his love of cooking, at which he excelled, but in the way this took him out of the fighting, so that his experience of war was as peaceful as might be. During it, he encountered but one corpse, that of an airman who had crashed his plane.

In contrast to the virtues, today's secular criteria of the good life are more outward oriented. Good health is essential and happiness the goal. Wealth, power, and success are thought major contributors, though their real worth is sometimes questioned. Completeness and balance are important elements, as are successful relationships, mainly with the other sex, but also with one's children.

Peter enjoyed good health to the end of his days. Happiness is an attribute whose nature is both secular and spiritual, for it is said that joy is an infallible sign of the presence of God. Was Peter happy? He was fun-loving and a great storyteller, but for him happiness must be differently defined. His consciousness of the spiritual world was the source of deep joy, but also of grief, for he felt how far the world around him departed from its perfection. Perhaps as a distraction, his idea of enjoyment was to fill life with as much activity as possible. In his early Air Force years in Britain, he would spend the four hours between the end of the workday and dinnertime successively in a game of tennis, a swim in the pool, cycling twelve miles to the horse stables, riding, then cycling back in time to bathe and change. He found a social outlet in dancing, at which he excelled. He had a sybaritic side and did not believe in suffering without cause. In India, his Burma Front headquarters were situated in the sweltering heat of Calcutta, and he had an extension cord rigged to his telephone, often conducting Command business from the swimming pool.

Of the other criteria, power is a second attribute whose nature is both spiritual and secular. Peter had power and learned how to relinquish it. One could argue with Peter, make objections, get him to change his mind. There was very little ego to get in the way when talking with him of matters affecting the community. Yet he breathed authority, and kept it cloaked like a wizard who points the way, but is sworn not to interfere. I realize now how difficult this was for him. Success he achieved in several spheres and was able to give those up too. Wealth he never sought, but always had sufficient for his and his family's needs.

Men of action often have difficulties with the affective side of their natures and Peter's five marriages suggest he was no exception. In his account of himself, he seems unaware of how his own powerful imagination may have manifested the outcomes he desired. Circumstances that another might interpret as temptation, he joyfully accepted as evidence of God's will, and acted accordingly. The man who emerges from his self-portrait is much more complex than would be supposed from his simple purpose of service. We catch glimpses of how at times the enormous personality that powered him chafed against the quiet obedience required by God's will.

One senses that the main element missing from Peter's life was a deep relationship with his children. For many years he had no contact with the son and daughter whom his first wife, Nora, bore him. I knew his three sons by Eileen, and I received the impression that Peter had not been a great presence in their lives, leaving their upbringing mostly to her. He was obviously trying to repair this omission with his last son Daniel, with whom Peter was about to share a vacation when a truck driver ran into his automobile and Peter was killed.

The themes of order and disorder interplay throughout Peter's life. We are accustomed to think of order as good, disorder as bad, but in Peter's case this is not so, rather each is a means of learning. In this connection, Rudolf Steiner's observations are relevant.[6] He emphasizes that the conflict between good and evil is not a simple duel. Evil is two-headed, comprising on the one hand order, cold, repressive, organized, and Satanic; and on the other disorder, fiery, wrathful, excessive, and Luciferic. The path of man's spiritual evolution, the Christ path, where "strait is the gate and narrow is the way," is the middle ground between.[7] At times during life's course that middle ground narrows till it seems there is but a choice of evils. If we can but hold steady, a gate will open and we cross a threshold, taking with us some of the evil from either side, and so redeem them. If Peter veered to one side or the other, it was never far, and he always returned to the path.

His life's final stage, described in his book by Renata, his last wife, carries more than a hint of the kingdom of heaven brought to earth. Friends describe Peter as a changed person, eager to engage and empathize, and radiating a calm joy which touched all those around him. But it seems that Peter was not wholly satisfied. Had he climbed his mountain as he had promised Sheena? The question became something of a joke among his intimates. One day, he surprised a questioner by answering, "Yes [he had climbed it]." A few days later, he was dead.

The mainspring of Peter's life was love, for he loved the God he served. This God is not one made familiar to us by conventional religion. He is the consciousness of the universe whose nature is to love and share, as he shared himself when he created man. We are the consciousness of this planet and have made it less than it should be. Because all levels of creation correspond, we are also the microcosm of the universe that is evolving past us. This God draws us to him, but we must change ourselves before we can know him.

Perhaps the best measures of a life are its outcomes. "Life lived well is a transformative art, and art is what we do for the love of doing it."[8] Peter's goal was to help transform the planet and he achieved it in the only way possible, by transforming himself, inspiring others to do likewise. It was not a balanced life, since it was running to and fro from order to disorder, and from success to failure to success. But it was complete. He climbed his mountain. Faith and courage were his outward hallmarks. He engaged with many and forgave and was forgiven.

For me, Peter Caddy's life illustrates how virtues evolve as time passes and the human being grows. Wisdom need no longer partner prudence, but join instead with love and its transforming power. Faith is raised from the sloughs where it had fallen, equated with belief, and becomes the means whereby we co-create with God. Happiness and success are natural outcomes.

TONY MITTON comes from Britain, where he read economics at Cambridge, worked in a family engineering business, sat on Birmingham's City Council, and twice stood for parliament. He lived for five years at the Findhorn Foundation, has traveled extensively, and speaks five languages. He now works as a planner for the state of Florida, and as a massage therapist for the mentally challanged and disabled.

Notes

1. Peter Caddy. *In Perfect Timing: Memoirs of a Man for the New Millennium.* Forres, Scotland: Findhorn Press, 1996.
2. *In Perfect Timing.* Op. cit. p. 20
3. Karma is a belief connected with reincarnation, teaching that we return to repair the effects of deeds done in previous lives.
4. The Findhorn Community. *The Findhorn Garden.* New York: Harper & Row, 1975.
5. Hebrews 11:1.
6. Rudolf Steiner. *Three Streams in Human Evolution.* Hudson, New York: Anthroposophic Press.
7. Matthew 7:14.
8. Normandi Ellis. Ba and Khu. *Parabola* 21:2, May 1996. p. 24.

GINNIE GOULET GAVRIN

Harvest

This will be my mother's last move.
No use to dig up the iris—
there won't be room for them
or the ivory plates
with the tiny gold-rimmed flowers
wreathed around the sides.

When summer ends, she will be gone
from this house, where her daughters
talk in the living room, decide
what to take and what to leave behind.

We sort through old pictures,
three little girls, smiling
in their pastel Easter coats.

How could they know who
would see that frozen moment?

Only ourselves. We could say
to them now: Don't be so afraid.
The future is nothing like
you were told it would be.

You will not be saved,
or discovered, or loved
by only one man.

There you stood for the camera,
the gold flux of fire
flashing behind your eyes
as you squinted blindly
into the sun, someone coaxing,
insisting: *Hold Still! Keep smiling . . .*

All there is to know:
that gold flame will consume you
and you will be glad.

GINNIE GOULET GAVRIN is a new writer living in Troy, New Hampshire, and finishing her first novel. One of her short stories will soon appear in the journal, *Primavera*.

LORAINE CAMPBELL

Pop's Church

Leah Olivier.
Pastel, 1997.

THE CHURCH WAS AN OLD ARMY TENT with wooden benches and saw-dust floors. The rain pounded the canvas roof, the wind howled, causing the canvas walls to tremble, and a creek roared by, biting off chunks of land as it went. In the winter, we children scrambled over each other in order to sit near the potbelly stove, and watch the big black chimney pipe turn red at the seams, when the fire blazed.

An old Victrola hooked up to an amplified speaker blasted the valley with music every Sunday morning. "There's power, power, wonder working power in the precious blood of the lamb."

My brother and I would dance down a dirt lane, humming, and wondering why bloody lambs had power.

Pop was the preacher, and we never called him anything else. It was mostly a children's church—Pop's Church. He was the founder, supporting the whole thing with his pension check.

Every Sunday morning, with fire in his pure blue eyes, he'd greet each child. He'd ask while shaking our hands—"What is God?"

"God is love," we'd say, having memorized the answer, and it was easy to believe when Pop was looking at your eyes, and holding your hand.

Sometimes we'd sit under the benches, while Pop's sermon was going on. He'd move felt figurines of camels, lions, wisemen, and mangers around on a large blackboard, while we built castles in the sawdust, and wound trails through each other's feet.

Every time Saul saw the light on his way to Damascus, the fire in the potbelly stove flared right up. When Daniel landed in the lion's den, it crackled. But when Jesus was born amongst all those animals, the fire always burned with a slow and steady glow.

Pop would wave his arms, and his voice would boom. He'd run around, peeking under the benches, and winking; or stand on a chair, and his voice would spill right through the seams in the canvas roof, and echo off the trees in the lane.

"When Gabriel blows the trumpet," he'd shout, "it'll mean the end of the world. And that trumpet will be the horn of a ram."

"I wonder if the ram will be bloody," my brother whispered to me one Sunday.

"Probably so," I said. "Rams are kinda like lambs, I think."

"They'll probably be a lot of dead bodies too," said my brother.

"Yeah," I whispered, "but don't worry. They'll all be sinners."

We sat there on the sawdust floor, looking at each other, trembling with excitement.

One winter Pop began digging a hole in the ground, right behind the tent.

"It's time to start baptizing," he said, "just like John the Baptist."

The hole quickly filled up with muddy water, and leaves and bugs floated on top, while worms crawled around the edge.

"You're not going to dunk us in that hole, are you?" I asked.

"I come," said Pop, setting down his shovel, and spreading his arms, "baptizing with water."

Then he picked up the shovel and went on digging.

"But—there might be snakes in there," I said.

Pop didn't stop.

"Poisonous snakes," I added.

Pop lined the hole with cement, and built some steps. The water stayed creepy though, even in the summer, when he used a garden hose to fill the hole. Nobody wanted to be baptized. Pop filled the hole with gravel, and moved the whole operation inside the tent.

Now we could be saved by touching a Bible and repeating after Pop: "Yes, I accept Christ as my personal Savior."

None of the kids wanted to do that either. We would have to stand in front of everyone, bow our heads, and of course, take a chance on being laughed at later.

Pop paced around the room, begging all sinners to repent. He looked up at the canvas ceiling, held his hands as if praying, and implored God to show him the way to save his little lost lambs. Tears ran down his face as he hopped around, waving a book, and shouting: "Just come up and touch this Bible, and you'll be saved from the fires of hell!"

Finally I jumped up and ran to the front of the tent. The whole business only took about three minutes, and I did feel as if all my sins had been washed away, and my heart was as pure as snow.

It seemed like a pretty good deal, considering that I hadn't been dunked in that hole, and was standing there, dry, and free from the fiery pit—that burns forever.

Pop hugged me, and recited from John 3:16: "For God so loved the world, that he gave his only begotten son—" Then he presented me with a shiny, black, leather Bible, with gold letters on the front. I walked back to my seat, with my head high, holding the Bible against my heart.

The next Sunday Pop started the whole thing all over again. "Just touch this Bible," he cried. A couple of older girls walked up and got saved. Then Pop's two grandsons were pushed forward by their mother. The oldest one, Johnny, mumbled quietly that—yes he accepted Christ as his personal—then he rolled his eyes like he'd seen a ghost. Just before Johnny's sins were washed away, he reached around Pop, and pinched his little brother. After Sunday school Johnny threw his Bible in the creek. He stood on the old wooden bridge, waved his arms like Pop, and shouted: "Bible old boy — you're getting baptized." The Bible plopped in the water and floated for a second before it sank. One big bubble rose to the top.

Several Sundays went by, and no one else felt inclined to be saved.

Then one Sunday morning in early spring, just as the prune trees were blooming, Pop held up a big box full of Hershey candy bars.

"Whosoever repents," his voice boomed, "and receives Christ into his heart, will also receive one of these here chocolate bars."

My brother jumped up, and so did the other kids. The entire congregation got saved that morning.

My brother walked back to our bench, smacking his lips. He slowly tore the wrapper off his candy bar, rattling the paper as loud as he could.

I watched.

He broke off one square, carefully, and ran it past my nose, before popping it into his mouth.

"Couldn't you share?" I asked.

"You got a Bible," he said.

"Well, I'll share my Bible."

"No way," he said, making a face. Then he smacked his lips, and bit off another square, rolling it around in his mouth a few times, and letting it melt slowly.

I watched him eat that candy bar. My eyes went up when his hand went to his mouth. My eyes went down when he held the rest of it in his lap. I looked around the tent at the other children eating chocolate, and wondered—would it be possible to be saved again? What if I said that a tiny little bit of sin had crept back into my heart?

Finally my brother had one square left, and he broke it in half, and gave a piece—the smallest piece—to me.

When summer came, lots of the kids stopped coming to church. Pop bought an old yellow school bus, and drove around the valley, banging on doors, arguing with parents, and begging children to come to Sunday school.

"But we've already been saved," some of them said. "We want to play now instead."

"Sufficient unto the day is the evil thereof," Pop muttered. Then he went out and bought several big boxes of Snickers candy bars.

On Sunday mornings, while the old Victrola blasted: "power, power, wonder working power—" he handed out Snickers to all the kids as they came in the front door. We got another one later, for every Bible verse we memorized.

I memorized long verses, and rattled them off for Pop, smiling, and standing tall.

One of his grandsons quoted a verse that only had two words: "Jesus wept," and he got a candy bar anyway; which didn't seem quite fair.

Attendance went way up after that, and Pop was hammering and sawing everyday, building more wooden benches. He saved a whole lot of young souls that summer.

LORAINE CAMPBELL lives in Seattle, where she is a student of astrology and of the Tarot.

MARGOT SCHILPP

Napping

this afternoon I lay on the sofa and dreamed
    of generations of peoples, all working hard,
        some harder than others, but everyone

harder than I. Take the Temple
    of the Magician, which must have been hell
        to construct there on that hot hill

at Uxmal, which means "three
    times built," so three times the work.
        I'd have made a bad Mayan. A bad

Egyptian, too, too lazy to measure each flood
    with a nilometer, and the more land
        that flooded, the more land was taxed.

And in Africa, I would have dehydrated,
    too lethargic to collect my salt cakes.
        I'm bad at drawing, so making portolan charts

to find harbors would have been out,
    as would illustrating manuscripts
        or temple columns or painting frescoes.

Even the cave paintings at Santimamine, just
    outlines, really, would have stretched
        my limited skill. I wouldn't have done well

carving mammoth bone into a fertility figure,
    or chert into a knife, and certainly that
        massive Giza project would have worn me down.

And, being a girl, I couldn't have worked there.
    I'd have, no doubt, been collecting winkles
        on the coast of Japan, filling a skin bag

with hot clay chunks to cook raw food,
    or roasting Bogong moths, all to feed
        myself and the family I'd have had.

But I don't see myself doing any of that.
    It's more my vision that I helped invent
        something: Linear B, a method for weaving

African palm frond mats, Greek coins,
    impressed brick, delicate ink, a way
        to harness fire, the wheel.

MARGOT SCHILPP's poetry has appeared in *The Gettysburg Review, The Green Mountains Review, River Styx, The Connecticut Review, Gulf Coast, High Plains Literary Review, Puerto del Sol, Verse,* and other journals. She is the editor of *Quarterly West.*

M. GARRETT BAUMAN

A Blue Ridge Mountain Christmas

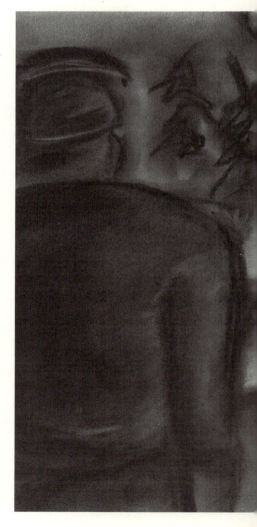

TO GET OUTSIDE, I MUST FORCE THE STORM DOOR OPEN through a heavy drift, shaving it flat. Snow hisses across the porch, and the temperature has inched down to sixteen degrees. The sky pinks, but across the valley are more storm clouds. Green Hollow Road will be drifted closed. Although I can hear the distant scrub of the plow, it won't clear back roads like ours until late afternoon. It may be longer until the electricity is restored.

The snow is virginal now, a lovely Christmas setting. As I take a quick look around the yard, I notice someone in the road. Mark? Has he hiked home from town? I grin and start down the drive. How did he even get to town? No, it's a stranger. The wind and snow fly against him so he appears like a kite about to rise. Head down, he zig-zags, staggers, and falls. He rises unsteadily and stumbles another few steps before going down in a heap. Who could it be up here! I run to our porch, then glance back. He hasn't moved. Inside the house, I latch the door and try to phone. Dead. From the window I watch the dark lump in the white expanse of road. Get up, I whisper. Get up and go on. He stirs like an exhausted swimmer half-willing to sink and sleep. The house accuses me with its silence, and I have no choice.

I jam on hat and gloves and tramp outside and down the drive. Snow has settled on the man's cap and back. In an hour he could be invisible. His face is raw, and a bare hand rests on the snow. No one else is in sight.

"Wake up," I say. No response. I shake his shoulder. He's thin, as empty as dry sticks. Again. He moans as though shrugging me off. "Hey! Wake up!" I shove him onto his side, and his eyes open. He pants, his tongue pink and steaming and his bony face whipped red from the wind. Gradually he focuses on me.

Amy Gardner. *A Blue Ridge Mountain Christmas.* Charcoal on bristol board, 14×8 inches, 1996.

"What's the matter?" I ask.

"I . . . I been walkin'." His voice is slow and far away, and with a chill I realize he'd have been unconscious within minutes if I hadn't come. Still, a part of me wishes I hadn't seen, hadn't known until afterward when it would be safely too late. "Walkin'," he repeats.

"In the blizzard?"

"I sleeped in a barn, up there."

"Crosby's?"

"Uh?" He braces to rise, but flops in the snow. I grasp his arm and haul him up. When he regains his balance, I let go.

"Why didn't you go in? They'd have helped you. It's Christmas."

"Nobody come." He begins to shiver in his soaked clothes.

"Are you hurt?"

"Naw. B-but Billy got to find the hospital. Aunt Lurice'll g-get m-mad," he pants. "She c-can't fly to F-Flor'da t-till Billy's s-safe away."

"What happened?"

In the immense quiet of the snow there is only Billy's nasal voice. "Aunt Lurice said t-turn down this here road an' Uncle B-Bob, he went in a d-ditch. He hollered at her."

"Are they stuck in the car?"

"Naw. Uncle Bob took her. Billy had to wait to w-wave at the t-tow man. He d-didn't come. B-Billy t-took short cut."

I survey the rolling waves of white. The main road is nearly a mile down, and Crosby's is barely visible a hundred yards uphill. Billy's too disoriented to hike, and our pick-up wouldn't even make the end of the driveway. "Let's get out of the wind," I say, "until I figure out how to return you. C'mon." Ponderously like a possum, Billy trudges behind me to our barn. There the temperature's nearly thirty. But even without wind, he shivers violently. I find him a blanket. What else can I do? No electricity, no phone, and the road blocked. I shouldn't let him in the house with Mark gone. Who knows who he is, where he's from. But he can't remain out here long—the battering cold has already made him look drugged.

"Wait here," I say. "I'll get help." I go inside the house and tell the children—who now percolate about their room—to stay upstairs, dress, and be quiet, that I will return in fifteen minutes to start Christmas. They whine giddily. I lock the house and flounder toward Crosby's through deep drifts. The wind buffets me from the valley side, and snow weasels under my scarf onto my neck. My legs feel rubbery by the time I'm there. No one's home! The pickup's buried in snow and the four-wheel drive Jeep isn't in the garage. They must have gotten out late last night to visit Warren's brother in town and not been able to return home. The next-nearest neighbor is almost a mile away at the bottom of the hill.

I glance back. Our weathered barn reposes stoically, unworried about storms or strangers. What now? Mark and I have vowed never to leave the children alone with the woodstove. But I can't bundle three- and six-year-olds for the mile hike through drifts to my waist. Do I point this Billy in the right direction and give him a hot thermos? I return home, tiring, resisting a decision. I think about how a few months ago I strolled down this road with the children picking dry wildflowers in the hot autumn sun. He should have come then, and all he'd need would be directions.

I open the barn door. He's not where I left him, and my heart flops. He conned me! He—I turn to rush to the house, then spot him burrowed in a mound of straw.

"I'm c-cold," he says.

Is this miserable wretch going to terrorize my children? He's half a baby himself. It's crazy to allow a stranger into your home, but if I let him get pneumonia or die, what would that be? I wish Mark would appear, but the cavalry is only for movies. I sigh. "Come on, Billy."

He crosses the yard with me, leaving a trail of straw. At the porch I brush more straw from him. We stamp inside. When the kitchen door slams, there is a mad stampede downstairs.

"You scamps!" I rush to the stairs.

Diana skids to a halt when she spots the gaunt, strawy man dripping in the dining room. Jeremy follows close behind, open-mouthed. He peers close. "Santa Claus?" he says skeptically. "*Dis* Santa?"

"No!" Diana says, "Santa Claus is fat!"

The children shy toward me under Billy's stare and hang on my knees. They won't look at Billy's face. Then Jeremy spots the chrome gleam of his rocking horse and takes a tentative step. The presents catch Diana's eye as well, and they rush to the tree. Billy shuffles after them like a grim shadow. Maybe if he dries out, he could hike—

Then I don't have time to think. Paper flies in all directions. When they squeal opening the treasures, I laugh too. I envy their innocence. Billy, who'd hung at the doorway, perks up and edges into the swirling chaos. When stray pieces of discarded paper come his way, he tears them to bits. There's a wild gleam in his eyes, as though the children's frenzy excites him, and the image of Mark's 22-caliber gun in the cellar-way crosses my thoughts. Have I read too many horror novels? Unwillingly, I rehearse what Mark taught me about the gun despite my protests last year. The box of shells is behind the canning jars. I shake my head. What kind of Christmas is this? Is Billy ruining it, or am I?

"Here, Mommy," Diana says, handing over a package. With Billy watching me, I lay aside the gift.

"Open," Billy insists.

"Later," I say with a polite nod.

"No, now." He pushes the box into my lap. "Now." I open it without looking. Is he going to get pushier as he thaws out?

The baby gives Billy a green package. "Dis for Santa Claus." Billy turns it over and fingers the folds, then rips it open. Inside is the ski cap I knitted for Mark. Billy slides off his sopped hat, revealing a receded hairline. He jams the bright red cap down over his ears, the tassel dangling in his face. "See!" he grins at the baby. "Billy Claus. Ho-Ho!" He gestures wildly, and his elbow catches a tree ornament, sending it flying. It smashes.

"Oh," the children cry. Billy curls into himself like a dog expecting a cuff.

"It was an accident," I say, wondering how often he's been hit and how he reacts to it. I pick up the curved glass shards. Subdued, Billy squats beside the presents. When I return from the trash, Billy's poking another unopened present. I try a warning stare, but he simply grins in that red cap and continues feeling the packages.

I boil water for hot cocoa, and I toast English muffins on the woodstove. Billy's coat slumps on the floor, and he struggles tugging off his boots. The room brims with his humid sweatiness. He looks clean, at least, but even maniacs can be clean.

"Billy's sorry about the ball," Diana says.

I wonder about the hospital he mentioned outside. He seems fine physically. Nor does he look dangerous swirling about the wrapping paper and sipping cocoa. So he paws our presents? But he could have made up that story about the car accident—or sent it out of control himself if they were taking him somewhere he didn't want to go. Was it clumsiness or wildness that broke the ornament? I don't know. I want to see clearly, but I don't know if I am. Suppose he's a bum. Maybe I should hike him to town right now.

I knead my hands and stare out at the white landscape. Trees and bushes are vague lumps under the snow. Remember him in the road, I tell myself. He wasn't even going to knock at the house. Look at his soaked clothes, his chapped skin. Don't be a begrudging Scrooge who half takes back what charity he gives.

I dig out some of Mark's old clothes. In a few minutes Billy emerges from the bathroom looking like a shrunken peanut in a shell, the pants bunched together at the waist, then ballooning out, the shirt hanging in great folds about his sinewy arms. He still wears the red cap, and in Mark's plaid shirt, he resembles a giant, famished elf. Without a word, Billy goes out onto the porch in his dry socks and hauls in a huge load of wood, piled so high I can barely see his elf hat over the top. He crashes into the doorway, staggers through the house, and thunders the logs into the woodbox beside the hearth. Wiping his hands, he grins. "There." He loads several dry logs into the stove with practiced ease.

"You've soaked your feet again," I say, sounding like his mother. Delicately, he picks snow from his socks and the rug, deposits the bits in a wastebasket, and settles in an armchair. The woodstove radiates drowsy comfort, and while the children root for toys scattered under wrapping paper, Billy dozes. Asleep, his long nose and stubbled chin seem to jut out farther. He looks frail, but a woman never knows. He must be thirty-five. Has he been in institutions all his life? All his Christmases? Shhh! I tell myself. You won't be careful if you get sentimental. Help him, but be careful first. I try the phone. Still dead.

"Billy!" Diana calls. "Billy, play with us."

"Shh!" I say. "Let him sleep."

I check the road for the Crosby's tracks every ten minutes. But no one's coming. Mark won't appear at the end of the drive, the Crosbys are warm at their relatives', and the plow can barely keep up with the main roads. Billy wakes when the house fills with the scents of dinner: sweet potatoes, corn, turkey legs, and gravy cooked on the woodstove and now steaming in the cool dining room. It looks cheerful, and I light the candles I'd bought. I'm rather proud of my improvisation, as though I've stolen back something from the cold.

Billy shambles in with the kids. Stabbing left and right, he piles his plate regally. It's upsetting to watch the way he jabs his fork. Yet he gulps milk like a teenage boy.

"Will your aunt and uncle worry about you?" I ask.

"Naw. They was taking me to Greyton. They'll get the police. I like police."

"Bang! Bang!" Jeremy says.

Billy solemnly draws an imaginary revolver and points it. "Bang, you're dead." My hands become liquid ice. Then Billy blows away the smoke and re-holsters his "gun," making Jeremy and Diana giggle. It was a well-honed act, that's all, something that always gets him laughs.

"You live at—Greyton all the time?" I ask, picturing the cement-walled "home" in the next county.

"Naw. Just Billy can't go Flor'da for the winter. Aunt Lurice says the alligators might eat him." He laughs as sane and knowing a laugh as I've ever heard. "If Billy was a alligator, Billy'd eat Aunt Lurice." He puffs his cheeks, and despite myself, I laugh.

"What's your name?" Billy asks.

"Leslie," I say, flustered. Have I really had him here four hours, grilled him for information, and not even introduced myself? "Leslie Yates."

"I like it here, Leslie," Billy says. "Nice hat and gravy. Maybe I'll stay, chop wood."

"Mark—my husband—"

"I like Billy Claus," Jeremy says, sliding from his high chair and toddling toward the presents.

"Me too," Diana says. "Billy Claus! C'mon Billy Claus."

Billy stares into his empty plate. "I got 'nother hat at Greyton," he says, fingering the tassel. The gesture warms me.

"Keep this one," I say.

"For real?"

"Yes. You probably don't get many presents at Greyton?"

His eyes widen. "Oh, Aunt Lurice give me twenty-five dollars an' a game, an' the church ladies, they bought us candy an' sweaters an' socks. 'Cept I lost one. An' Harold, he buyed me stuff." He bites his lip and looks down, squeezing his hands. His nervousness surprises me. "I stay today, ok? Here."

"Billy Claus!" Diana calls. "We need a horse."

Beyond Billy's silhouette the sky darkens as new snow gathers. The cold will linger, and this afternoon the drifts will climb higher. Who knows when the plow will arrive? Perhaps not until tomorrow morning. Out there through miles of storm, Mark must be looking east wishing he were home. I hope he's well-fed and warm.

"Yes, stay," I tell Billy. "The children are waiting for you."

M. GARRETT BAUMAN is an English professor in upstate New York. His good life began, he says, when he met his wife, Carol.

RAYMOND WONG

Precious Jade

HER NAME WAS YU-CHI, PRECIOUS JADE. I first met her in Chungking, wartime capital of China. I was a World War II correspondent attached to the headquarters of General Joseph Stilwell, commander of the United States forces in the China-Burma-India theater. Yu-chi was a Chinese Red Cross worker. It was a beautiful early spring day. Suddenly I saw giant red balloons on the watch towers. An air raid was coming.

Sirens whined. Carrying whatever they could, people ran in panic for the nearest dugouts. Within minutes, the streets were deserted. I rushed with my colleagues to our own underground shelter. We sat silently on long wooden benches against the cold, damp concrete walls. The ground shook and the dim lights blinked as the bombs exploded overhead.

The raid was savage but swift; it was over in less than an hour. After the all-clear, I ventured into the streets with my press camera. Dark smoke rose all around. Most of the homes and buildings were made of wood or bamboo, and the flames spread like forest fires, consuming everything. The air was filled with the sound of collapsing buildings, screaming ambulances and fire trucks, and the cries of the wounded and dying. Several looters were executed on the spot by the military police.

Shen Chou. *Landscape.* Ming Dynasty hand-scroll, ink and colors on paper, 100³/₈×6⁵/₈ inches, fifteenth century. Asian Art Museum of San Francisco. The Avery Brundage Colection. Accession Number B75 D7.

As the day grew dark, I picked my way through the ruins toward the center of town where major fires had been brought under control and partial order restored. I saw a Chinese Red Cross tent and a mob jostling for medicine and food. A young woman in a blue Red Cross uniform was directing workers handing packages to the hundreds of outstretched hands. Moving closer, I took a picture of the young woman. Seeing the flash, she stepped down from the platform. The crowd, looking at me, let her through.

"Ni wei shenme zhaoxiang?" (Why are you taking the pictures?) she asked in Mandarin. Her face was stern, her tone not very friendly. I told her it was for news coverage. She stared at my GI uniform and Press badge.

"Are you Chinese?" she asked.

"I'm a Chinese-American, a U.S. war correspondent," I said. Hesitantly, I asked her for an interview. To my surprise, she started speaking fluent English.

"I am very busy, as you can see. I am afraid you will have to wait for another time."

"When will it be convenient for you?"

"Perhaps sometime next week, if there is no air raid."

"Next Monday?"

She thought for a moment. "No, Monday is always a bad day," she said. "How long is the interview going to be?"

"About half an hour."

"All right, make it next Wednesday."

"What time?"

Again, she paused. "I come to work at seven in the morning; nine o'clock?"

"Fine. What is your name, ma'am?"

"Chu Yu-chi. My office is in the basement of the Red Cross Building."

THE BUILDING WAS BADLY SCARRED BY THE BOMBINGS. On Wednesday I was shown to Miss Chu's office in the basement.

"Good morning, Mr. Li," she greeted me, rather formally. "Please have a seat, I will be right back."

I looked around. The small room was cluttered with bookshelves and paper boxes. Maps and charts covered the walls. Piles of papers were scattered on her desk next to a telephone and an oil lamp. The electricity was still out, but a small grate just below the ceiling let in some sunlight.

Miss Chu returned and sat behind her desk. "Well, what would you like to talk about?" she asked.

I asked about her position with the Red Cross.

"We have several regional offices under an executive director. I am in charge of the operations here," she said.

"That must be a very demanding job. Are there many women in such high positions?"

"You mean in the Red Cross?"

"No, I mean in general."

"Frankly, no. This is still a man's world."

"I don't think any man could have done a better job than you handling that crowd after the bombing the other night," I told her.

"Thank you. I wish I could do more. It was terrible."

"You speak excellent English," I remarked.

"English was my major in college. I also studied political science."

"How did you end up with the Red Cross?"

"The war. So many refugees. Here is the chance to put what I have learned to work."

"Where do you get the money to operate?"

"From overseas. We get our medical supplies from the International Red Cross. With all the bombings and the war in Europe, the supplies don't come regularly. We are short on everything. Most of our workers are volunteers; they don't get paid."

"No help from the government?"

"Are you kidding? It will be a great help if they just leave us alone."

"What do you mean?"

"The story you said you are going to write, will it be published in America?"

"Yes."

"Then, tell your readers, if they really want to help the Chinese people, send their relief to us directly through the International Red Cross. Don't send it to the government. There are too many crooks in the government at all levels, but especially at the top. They sell your stuff in the black market for profit instead of helping the people."

I knew of the corruption of Chinese government officials; still, her frankness surprised me. She looked so young, as if in her mid-twenties. It was unusual for a woman of that age to hold a high position in China. It must be because of her linguistic ability, I thought. She had soft features and a smooth, fair complexion. Her long wavy hair was parted in the middle and hung over her shoulders. When she was not speaking, her beautiful dark brown eyes conveyed much feeling.

We talked a while longer about her work, the war, and the armed clashes between the Nationalist troops and the Red Army.

Finally I said, "You know, when I first met you at the relief center that night, I thought you were harsh and a bit bureaucratic."

For the first time, she smiled, showing two attractive dimples. I wished I could stay longer, but she had work to do.

I asked, "May I see you again? Perhaps we could have dinner together."

"Maybe. We'll see. They told me the telephone should be working in another day or two. Give me a call," she said softly.

SUNSHINE THE NEXT FEW DAYS. Nervously the city braced itself, but the planes did not come. The pace of life picked up a bit amidst the ruins and destruction. While I was working, the beautiful face of Yu-chi lingered in my mind. I had met her but twice, yet her voice, her smile, clung to my heart. I longed to see her again. A week later I called her at work and asked if we might have dinner somewhere. How happy and excited I was when she said yes! She told me to meet her at her home at six.

She lived in a small two-story apartment house. She was waiting in the doorway when I arrived. Dressed in a shapely blue Chinese gown and a white cotton jacket, she looked completely feminine.

"You look gorgeous," I said.

"Thank you." She looked at me and smiled as she climbed into the jeep which I had washed and cleaned for the occasion. "Any particular place you want to go?" she asked.

"No. How about you?"

"I don't eat out very often. Let's just drive around; some restaurants must be open," she said.

The streets were scarred with potholes; many buildings lay in ruins or were boarded up. We found a restaurant, but there were few customers. The waiter showed us to a private booth in the back of the room and took our order. Just a few simple dishes.

"Do you mind if I call you Tom?" she asked while I was pouring her some hot tea.

"Of course not, please do," I said. "Now, what shall I call you? I don't want to call you Miss Chu all the time; too formal."

"Call me Yu-chi."

"What does Yu-chi mean?"

"Precious jade."

While we were eating, she asked if this was my first visit to China. I said yes.

"What do you think of it?"

"Well, so far," I said, "I've only been to two places, here and Kunming. I like the country but feel sorry for the people; they are suffering so much from the war."

"They suffered long before the war. The landlords exploited them. The government oppressed them. The tax collectors and corrupt officials squeezed them. The marauding bandits robbed them. On top of that, nature added its toll—flood, drought, and epidemics. You are from America; you have only seen the surface of China. The Americans think they are helping a great ally; they don't know about the corruption of the government, the tyranny of the military, and their oppression of the people. You are a reporter; tell them the truth."

She was so outspoken, I began to worry for her. General Stilwell had once told me that there was no real freedom in China; many had been jailed, some were even killed for criticizing the government. I told her to be careful and promised to send the message home, though not by the regular channel; all foreign press releases were censored by the government. What made it even more difficult was that the United States supported the Chinese Nationalists in a war against a common enemy.

"How long are you going to stay?" she asked.

"I don't know. I can be sent anywhere, anytime."

For a moment, she rested her eyes on me. "I am glad we met," she said in a low voice. I felt something in my heart drawing her close to me.

"Do you speak Chinese at all?" she asked, after a brief silence.

"Some. I went to a language school in California."

"Talk to the people, not government officials. See with your own eyes why so many people have gone over to the Communists. China is changing; the world is changing. This is a great moment in history. Write a story about your experience here. Send me a copy."

I looked at her. In that brief moment, I pictured myself writing late at night by the fireside in a cozy room with her sitting by my side.

"Which part of China are you from?" I asked.

"I was born in Suzhou but grew up in the north, Peking."

No wonder she was so beautiful, I thought. I had been told that Suzhou was known for its beautiful women.

"Are your parents here with you?"

"My father died a few years ago," she said. "My mother is living with my elder sister and my brother-in-law, still in Peking."

"No brothers?"

"One, my younger brother. He is in the army."

"Where is he stationed?"

"Somewhere in Burma, being trained by the Americans."

"General Stilwell?"

"Yes, he is the commander."

"I know the general; I've interviewed him several times. He's an unusual person, the first American to command a Chinese army."

"You must have lived an interesting life, traveling to so many places and talking to so many people," she commented. "Tell me, in America, do they treat you as American or Chinese?"

"Both, because I am both."

"Any girlfriends?"

"One."

"Chinese?"

"Yes. Want to see her picture?"

She shrugged her shoulders. I took out a picture in an envelope from my pocket and showed it to her. It was the picture I took of her the other night.

"Oh, you!" she laughed as she looked at the picture, caught by complete surprise.

"Her name is Yu-chi, Precious Jade."

"You love to kid people, don't you?"

"I'm not kidding. She's the loveliest lady I've ever met."

She lowered her eyes and looked at the picture. "May I keep it?"

"Sure. I brought it for you."

The waiter came to warm up our tea. Most of the customers had left; the restaurant was about to close.

"It's late, soon there will be curfew," said Yu-chi. After paying the bill, I drove her home. I escorted her to the doorway of the apartment house. I held her hand and bade her good-night. How I wanted to hold her close and kiss her! But I refrained. They frowned on open displays of affection in China.

THE SUMMER WAS HOT AND HUMID IN CHUNGKING. The enemy resumed its terror from the sky, but people seemed to have become used to it. Whenever possible, Yu-chi and I would get together. Our favorite place was the only park in town. We would stroll along the lake or sit on a bench under a willow tree. She introduced me to several of her friends and co-workers. Among them was Mrs. Wong, her assistant. They had been childhood friends and attended the same college. After Peking fell to the Japanese, they escaped to the south together.

Our headquarters had a party at the officers' club to celebrate the Fourth of July. I invited Yu-chi. She came dressed in a pink silk blouse and a white pleated skirt, wearing a pearl necklace and matching earrings. After dinner, a four-piece band played dance music. I hadn't danced since I came overseas. She told me that neither had she for a long time. But she danced well, better than I. The only dance she did not know was the jitterbug. I showed her how—tap and turn, twist and swing. She loved it. She was kept busy all evening; my friends would ask her to dance when she was not dancing with me. In the midst of the music, the relaxed atmosphere, and the friendly faces, the war became remote. I was drawn ever closer to Yu-chi. Whether we were dancing on the floor or sitting at our small table with our drinks by the candlelight, hers was the only face I saw among all others, beautiful, serene, endearing. Sometimes she gazed at me, tenderly, without words. Time slipped by. Too quickly, the enchanted evening came to its end. When the lights dimmed and the band played *Goodnight, Ladies,* we danced our last dance. She nestled closely in my arms as we slowly glided around the floor.

SOON THE SUMMER WAS GONE. Once again, the wartime capital was safe from air raids as dense fog blanketed the sky. The war was so close, yet so far. In Europe, allied troops had landed in Normandy. In the Pacific, U.S. Marines had landed in Guam. I was kept busy reporting news from China. Here the major stories were not about the war between China and Japan, which had been relatively quiet on all fronts, but about the brewing civil war between the Nationalists and the Communists. One late afternoon I was in my room writing when I heard a knock on the door. It was Mrs. Wong, Yu-chi's friend, standing outside when I opened the door. She appeared to be very nervous. As soon as I invited her in and closed the door, she told me Yu-chi was in trouble and needed help.

"What happened?" I asked.

"No time to talk. I came on bus. Yu-chi said I find you here. I tell you later. Must go quickly," said Mrs. Wong.

"Where is she?"

"My home, with my husband."

I headed straight for the parking lot. On our way, Mrs. Wong told me what had happened.

"Miss Chu don't like Chinese government. Chinese government don't like her. They want arrest her," she said.

"Arrest her? For what?" I was shocked.

"They say she Communist."

"What? Miss Chu a Communist? Who told you?" I couldn't believe my ears.

"I no can tell who told me, but I know why."

"Go on, why?"

"I know Miss Chu, Yu-chi, long time. She good friend. She not Communist. She work hard; good boss. Red Cross get medicine from America. Yu-chi told me Chinese government officers want her give some medicine to them to sell in black market. She not give. They tell her bad thing will happen if she don't give them medicine. I told her be careful, tell Red Cross boss. But she not afraid. She said she will tell newspaper. Now they will arrest her tonight after . . . after no walk on street . . ."

"You mean curfew."

"Yes, curfew."

"Who's going to arrest her?"

"Secret service men and police. They watch her home. I told her not go home, they will arrest her tonight after curfew. She not believe me. I call my friend. He told her on telephone and she believed. She has some things in a small suitcase in office for air raid. She take that with her."

"How did you get her out of the Red Cross?"

"Red Cross not watched. They want arrest her from her home. We come out back door to my home in rickshaw."

"Will she be safe in your home?"

"Not long. They will find her. She must go away."

"Where to?"

"She tell you."

With my nerves on edge, I kept on driving till we reached the foot of a hill on the other side of town. There she told me to stop. I followed her into a small bungalow behind a cluster of trees.

Yu-chi was waiting. The moment she saw me, she jumped up from her seat and ran toward me. "Will you take me away from here before they put their dirty hands on me?" she cried.

"But where to?"

"Lintu, a small town about sixty *li* from here. There is a Catholic church; two of my close friends are nuns. It is a sanctuary, they will protect me. I can also help them with their work. I will be safe there."

I was not prepared for this; things happened too suddenly. Lintu? I had never heard of that place before. And wouldn't the American Embassy right here in Chungking be safer? But then, the United States and China were allies, they might not grant her refuge.

"Will you, Tom?" she pressed for an answer. Suddenly an idea came to me. "Yu-chi, why don't we get married. You told me you will marry me when that day comes. That day is now. They cannot touch you if you are the spouse of an American citizen. We can be married tomorrow by our chaplain; I'll arrange that. We'll fly back to the States and forget about this nightmare," I pleaded with her, holding her hands firmly in mine.

Her eyes were wet. But she shook her head. "No, Tom, no. I love you far too much to get you involved in this. I want our wedding day to be the happiest day in my life, not a back alley escape route."

"But . . ."

"Say no more, Tom," she stopped me. "Just remember, I love you. I will write to you. The war will soon be over; the Nationalists will move back to Nanjing far away from here and no one will remember me. I will come to you and we will be together the rest of our lives living in peace and happiness. But now is not the time. There will be curfew in a few hours; please hurry. We must leave now so that you can get back before the curfew."

She stood there, unshaken and determined. Mrs. Wong and her husband looked at both of us. The room was silent; I could hear the ticking of the clock on the wall. What else could I say or do except to take her to Lintu as she insisted.

To get out of town, we had to pass through a checkpoint. It was at the foot of a brick tower guarding the exit to the highway. The top of the tower had been blown up by bombs, only the bottom half remained standing. A soldier with a rifle slung over his shoulder came out of the guardhouse when I stopped. I showed him my credentials, including a safe-conduct pass for the press issued by the Ministry of Information and Security. The guard examined the papers under a flashlight. Apparently satisfied, he handed me back the documents and turned his flashlight on Yu-chi's face. He wanted to see her ID. I held my breath.

Yu-chi was calm. She said something to the guard which I didn't understand; then, she took out some money from her purse and put it in his hand. The guard let us through.

"What did you tell him?" I asked after we got on the narrow highway.

"I told him I am a street girl and I have no ID. I knew he wanted money," said Yu-chi.

"How much did you give him?"

"A hundred *yuan*. He probably has seen enough prostitutes hanging around with American soldiers."

"Really, Yu-chi, I am worried. I don't suppose I can change your mind?"

"Don't worry, Tom. I told you I will be safe."

The so-called highway was just a narrow two-way road, badly paved and maintained. There was hardly any traffic at this late hour. We passed by a few scattered villages. As we neared Lintu, we drove up a winding mountain path, guided only by our headlights. The engine labored uphill. Lintu at last. I could see the bell tower of the church from a distance. The little town was totally deserted. We stopped at the black iron gate to the churchyard. I turned off the engine and the headlights. It was dark and quiet. For a few moments, we sat silently in the jeep. Suddenly she reached over and pressed her lips on mine. "Tom, we must say good-bye now. Don't get out of the car; I want to go there alone. Thank you for taking me here. I will be thinking of you, always." She wept.

I felt a lump in my throat. What made her so resolute, taking this route? Why was she resisting what could have been a happy ending for both of us? I sat in the jeep and watched her walk toward the church, her small suitcase in her hand. She never looked back. When she reached the gate, she knocked. A moment later, a light was turned on and the gate was opened, first just a crack, then wide. A nun in black habits embraced her. In another moment, the gate closed. She was gone.

MRS. WONG CAME TO SEE ME. She told me she had been questioned by the secret service agents and warned me not to do anything which might lead them to Yu-chi's hiding place.

Two tormenting weeks passed, trying days, sleepless nights. One afternoon I was in my office working on a report when I had another visitor, a Catholic priest. He was a Caucasian dressed in a black suit with a white collar.

"Are you Mr. Li?" he asked.

"I am Father Zweig," he introduced himself. " I've just come from Lintu. I have been asked to bring this to you personally." He handed me a blank, sealed, white envelope. I was caught by surprise. I asked him to please sit down and quickly opened the envelope.

My dearest Tom:

It is now two o'clock in the morning. I could not sleep. I think of you, day and night. I wanted to write to you much sooner than this but was afraid it might fall into the wrong hands if I sent it by regular mail.

I miss you, Tom, terribly. It is a different world here in the sanctuary, quiet, serene, and peaceful. It gives me a chance to think and meditate. I am not a religious person, but behind these walls I find peace and, for the first time, feel the presence of the spiritual world. My friends asked me to stay; but I cannot hide forever in seclusion and I must not allow myself to indulge in their kindness. I have decided to leave. There is work to be done. China must change or she will fade into history. I have seen the corruption and decay of the Nationalists; I want to see if there is hope on the other side. I am not a Communist and never have been. But if they are for the good of the common people, I don't want to be a bystander. My work is to help the people; it crosses political lines.

Please do not worry, Tom. I know you love me and I love you more than I can ever tell you in words. But we all have our share of work to do. I can never be at peace with myself until I have done my share. Someday we will meet again, here in China or across the ocean in America. When the sun sets in China, it rises over America; when the sun sets in America, it rises over China. There is but one sun as I have but one love. My love will follow you in the evening glow of sunset or the early dawn of sunrise. If I should perish, God will reunite us in another world, another time. Take care of yourself, my dearest, my love. I will write to you; I have your address in America. I will come to you when the war is over and China takes her rightful place among nations.

—YU-CHI

I read the letter twice. Father Zweig sat there patiently waiting.

"Miss Chu said in her letter that she is leaving the church. Please don't let her go," I pleaded with the Father.

"She has already left two days ago. Once she made up her mind, no one could stop her. We tried," said Father Zweig.

My heart sank. "Did she say where she was going?"

"No. She was very bitter about the government and the way she was treated. I presume she is going to the Communist side, like so many others."

Still holding the letter in my hand, I stared blankly at the wall. "Miss Chu is a brave and a very idealistic woman; may God be with her and protect her wherever she goes . . ." I heard the priest say. His voice grew faint while in my mind's eye I saw Yu-chi, Precious Jade, wandering in the mountains, alone and bewildered. My heart flew out to her, but she disappeared. When Father Zweig rose from the chair, I was brought back to the moment at hand. I thanked him for bringing me the letter, and he left.

I WENT TO SEE MRS. WONG AT THE RED CROSS, hoping she might have some idea where Yu-chi could possibly have gone. She was shocked that Yu-chi had left the church, but could tell me nothing new. I drove to Lintu again and talked with the nuns. They were just as worried and helpless as I about their friend. I even contacted our own intelligence people and the U.S. Embassy, thinking they might have a magic wand pointing to Yu-chi's trail. But, of course, I was disappointed. In fact, the deputy consul told me to stay out of Chinese politics.

In the midst of my frustration and helplessness, I was transferred to Kunming near the Burma border. The American trained and equipped Chinese army had just launched a large-scale offensive against the Japanese along the Burma Road, and I was sent there with several other war correspondents and photographers to cover the frontline news. We crawled through jungles and lived in tents, following the troops and fighting the mosquitoes. At the end of each day, I thought of Yu-chi. I cursed the mountains, the rivers, and the vast empty space separating us. I cried for her, but she could not hear me. I dreamed of her, only to wake up with a heavy heart. I would not hesitate a moment to drop everything to be by her side, if only I knew where she was.

My new assignment did not last long. The atomic bomb was dropped on Hiroshima. Another one fell on Nagasaki. Japan surrendered; the long, bloody war came to an end. Overnight, everything changed. No more air raids; no more battle news to report. The Americans were packing, ready to go home. I flew back to Chungking; my tour of duty, too, ended.

It was late September. As usual during this time of year, dense fog covered the city. Chungking, too, was on the move. Government offices, schools, factories, businesses, and the refugees driven here by the war, all were now ready to leave. Like the Americans, they too were packing for a long journey home.

While the world cheered the new dawn of peace, the civil war in China had just begun. The Nationalist troops, airlifted by U.S. planes, quickly reoccupied the cities and strategic points south of the Yangtze River and were pushing north. Likewise, the Red armies lost no time sweeping across the northern plain and Manchuria. Yu-chi was somewhere out there in this troubled land.

On the eve of my departure, I strolled along the streets and gazed upon familiar sites—the Red Cross building on Chungshan Street, the headquarters where I had worked, the officers' club where Yu-chi and I had spent an enchanted evening, and Yu-chi's apartment house in the alley. I stopped by the lake in the park. Now few people were there. I picked up a pebble from the ground and tossed it into the lake. Watching the ripples and the spreading rings over the top of the water, I saw the quivering reflection of Yu-chi's face. Several reddish autumn leaves fell on the still surface of the lake. All had changed, only memories lingered.

AS THE U.S. PLANE ASCENDED, I looked out the window at the cloud-shrouded mountain peaks below, recalling the night I proposed to Yu-chi, Precious Jade, at the mountain resort. I saw a glimmer of sunshine through the mist far across the cloudy sky; the sound of the engines faded into silence. I was going home; but I had left my heart in my ancestral land.

RAYMOND WONG is a retired civil engineer and former editor of a San Francisco City Hall magazine. He is currently pursuing a master of arts degree in creative writing at San Francisco State University.

Invitation:
Write
to
Chrysalis Reader

In connection with what you do with what you get—we would be very grateful if you, our readers, would write and tell us how you read this book you have in your hands. (Examples: All at once? One story at a time? At bedtime?) And if, or how, some of the stories, essays, and poems appealed to you. Have you suggestions for future themes?

—THE EDITORS
Crysalis Reader, 320 North Church Street,
West Chester, Pennsylvania 19381

PART III

What You Do with What You Get

One evening I was sitting on a bench in the Jardin in San Miguel. Something made me look up. "You don't remember me." It was Don José, who had once lived in my house for many days. He taught me much. I don't remember what he taught me. He said I would not, but that his teachings were inside me and would guide me whenever I needed.

AFTER THE BEGINNING, AND THE TURNING AROUND, Swedenborg saw the next stage as Changing Ourselves, paralleling God's forming and populating our natural environment. Where the first stage requires searching, and the second requires courage, this phase requires work. The psychic work of "Laws of Physics," enduring the punishment of "Dancing Lights," the physical work pervading "First Pressing," the birthing in the "Sky Meadow Stories," the mental work of grappling with the abstractions fleshed-out by William Marsh—fulfilling the promise of our new direction takes concentrated, persistent, patient work.

No one of us can choose the race, gender, status, power, or other attributes with which we begin the process; but each of us, alone, can determine whether we will exert the effort to stay the course between our beginning and our goal. What we do with what we get depends as much on what we put into the process as on the direction that we choose.

As different aspects of our lives turn around from new beginning points, we change ourselves and become new in repeated and often overlapping cycles. The labor of self-change, in fact, is the dominant characteristic of living; so it is a precious blessing that much of the time we find the work enjoyable as well as rewarding.

HOLLY FUHRMANN

Laws of Physics

I DREAMED OF A WOMAN I KNEW, but couldn't place—a nightmare, if you will. The woman's face peered through the window of my house, and though I couldn't really see her, I could sense she was hungry, aching, searching. Her features were blurred in the darkness. I opened the door and called to her.

"What do you want," I asked of the darkness that rushed to surround me, barely held at bay by the faint light that spilled past the open door.

A whisper, so faint that at first I couldn't be sure I heard it, was my only answer. "I want what you have."

"And what is that?" The voice sounded achingly, tragically familiar and chilled me.

"You live in a palace, in warmth, in light, in summer. You live in a palace, and I live in hell."

"I've heard that hell is hot, so why do you envy my warmth?" I still could not see her, only hear her and sense her presence just beyond the light of the open door.

"That is a myth, a story started by some fool, some misguided soul with no idea of the truth of things. Hell is a place so cold your blood crystallizes in your veins. Hell is the deepest part of winter, when everything lies frozen, barren, dead. And the hellish part of it all is there is no hope for rebirth, no hope for the coming spring—only eternal, endless Hell. It is a place that sits in the shadows of heaven, so close we who reside there can see all that we are missing. We see your flames, your laughter, your light. All the while we watch, hidden in the cold darkness, fearing, yet longing for it all."

"And if you want it so badly why don't you step into the light and claim it for yourself?"

"Did you ever take a science class?" The hoarse whisper was closer now.

"Science class?" A croak, that is what my voice was reduced to as fear began to choke and smother me.

"In science there was a theory we all learned. 'For every action there is an equal and opposite reaction.' Ever heard that one?" The rasping whisper was louder, though not a normal speaking voice. It was laced with a brittle anger that struck me like a fist.

It was moving closer.

I nodded mutely. The light from the doorway must have been enough to illuminate my movement because the whisper continued as my heart raced.

"Well, if your name is Action, that would make me Reaction—doomed here to eternal darkness while you feast on the light and the warmth of heaven. I think it's time to discuss a trade."

At that moment I could make out a shadow forming just beyond the ring of light that shone on the porch. My scream woke me up.

Sitting on the bed, sweat drenching my body, I trembled. It was too real, too tangible, too terrible to be a mere dream. It was something—something more. I knew the voice, knew the shadow that en-

Kenneth Keith Forbes. *The Yellow Scarf.* Oil on canvas, 51.1 × 61.3 cm., 1924. Toronto: Art Gallery of Ontario. Gift of the Canadian National Exhibition Association, 1965.

croached. But like a word stuck on the tip of my tongue—I could taste it, but not touch it.

In the light of the following days, the dream seemed to blur, to lose some of its intensity. I put it away, tried to hide from it, from her. Some nights I heard her whisper, sensed her looking with longing on me, but I hid the fear each day. I went back to the business of life and forgot questions of heaven and hell and disembodied whispers.

She grew more insistent. I couldn't forget, try as I might. She would not be barricaded. The dream haunted my day, forcing me to begin to look for an answer. She was drawing closer.

I tried the Bible, bought a book on dreams—they didn't help. Finally the answered dawned on me, she'd given me a clue. That evening, sitting in a chair before the fire, I studied an old physics book. I knew the answer was there, if only I could find it before sleep claimed me and I met her again. Frantically I searched, my eyelids growing heavier and heavier with each passing moment. At last there it was, I smiled. The answer was painfully simple.

That night, as I slept, the woman's shadowed face peered through the window of my house. This scene was familiar, I thought. A smile touched my lips where once there was terror. I couldn't really see her, but I could still sense her hunger, her ache, her search—the difference between the terror and the calm was the knowing. Tonight I knew what she wanted from me. I retraced my path to the door, playing my role. "What do you want?" I called.

"I want what you have."

"And what is that?" The dialogue echoed true to form. A second chance.

"You live in a palace . . ." I let the dream play through until she asked, "Did you ever take a science class?"

"Of course I had a science class, though as I recall it wasn't my best subject. But, you know me, never throw out a book. You never know when it might come in handy."

"What are you babbling about?" The hoarse whisper had grown in volume, irritation tinged her voice.

"Inertia, my friend, that's what I'm babbling about." I took a step off the porch that brought me to the edge of my light. "Inertia," I whispered.

She stood just beyond the light at the edge of the darkness. We were so close I could feel her breath on my face and just make out the whites of her eyes as they widened in surprise. My hand reached out slowly as I told her, "Inertia is a property of matter that causes it to resist any change of its motion in either direction or speed."

My hand continued its forward motion as I explained. "An object at rest tends to stay at rest just as an object in motion tends to continue in a straight line unless . . ."

My hand gently caught her wrist. It was cool to the touch, but not unpleasant, not terrible—not death. I pulled her gently towards the light as I finished. "Unless acted upon by an outside force."

I pulled, and she fell into the faint light that spilled through my open door. I was looking in a mirror, a face I knew so well, though it was younger and afraid. I pulled this frightened child into my open arms.

"Welcome home, little sister," I sighed in her ear as I hugged her, rocking her gently to and fro.

"You came for me at last," she sobbed as I rocked her. So long ago I had locked this child out, trying to block all the memories that she held. They haunted and hurt me time and time again. I wanted to build a life without the darkness.

I couldn't rid myself of her entirely, couldn't exorcise the memories she carried—so I had locked her out. I had left her there as I climbed over her body into the light I had seen. Inert—she was unable to move until some outside force provided the momentum, and I was unable to go further into the light while she still held the darkness around my haven. I stayed in my house, warm though it was, surrounded by hell, haunted by shadows that chased me.

I rocked the woman-child as I mumbled nonsense words of comfort into her ear. She cried, her tears soaked my shoulder, and still I rocked her, embraced all the painful memories that returned with her. I saw they were only memories that held no power, and as I realized that, I laughed through my tears, and she joined me. "Come into the house," I invited her. "Come into the warmth and leave the darkness, the past behind."

I walked up the stairs, and she followed. "We have a lot to talk about," I said, warming myself in the light of the present, in my, our, little corner of heaven. The sun began to rise over the horizon, our first sunrise.

HOLLY FUHRMANN says she is a fledgling author who is thrilled to have sold twenty pieces of her short fiction to date. Her first book, *A Snowball's Chance,* was released by Neighborhood Press in June 1997.

TREVA MYATT

Generations

We have been cheated, my mother and I
And my sisters and our children, too.

When she sees me now she stares at me,
knowing that I belong to her somehow.
She does not speak, she has forgotten my name.
Once she wore makeup and piled her hair
high on her head.
Now her face is well-scrubbed
free of makeup,
her hair short and thin.

I have this memory:
A phone call, her voice breaking.
Dad died, she said.
We wept that night,
but in the morning she had her hair done,
and my sisters and I went shopping
to buy her a lavender dress—
she would not wear black.
She held her head high; she was magnificent.

As the months passed she became more confused.
She forgot dates; she forgot how to tell time.
On one of my last visits
before she went into the care center,
I sat down at the piano
to get away from her constant stream of words,
aware that she was talking to convince me

that all was normal.
We both knew it was not.

I went into the kitchen to get a glass of water
and she took my place at the piano.
After a few fumbling chords
there came a stream of beautiful, clear music.
It lasted a minute,
then faded away to hesitation and wrong notes;
slowly, agonizingly, it faded.
I stood in the kitchen and wept.

Mom, there is so much I never told you.
Most of all that I now understand many things,
things you tried to tell me that I had no patience for.
And I think of you
when my daughters smile patronizingly at me
and go their own way.

TREVA MYATT has been nominated as Poet of the Year for 1997 by The International Society of Poets. Her work has appeared in *Grit, Satire, Western Pockets, Hellas, The Formalist, Sensations, Treasure House, The Midwest Poetry Review, Vermont Ink, Poetry Digest, The Connecticut Review, Eclectic Rainbows, Feelings, Poetic Eloquence,* and *Candlelight.*

A Real Life

F. H. Varley. *Dhârâna.*
Oil on canvas,
101.6 × 86.4 cm.,
ca. 1932.
Toronto: Art Gallery
of Ontario. Gift from the
Albert H. Robson
Memorial Subscription
Fund, 1942.

MY MOTHER'S DEMENTIA had started when I was in high school. Now with Alzheimer's disease, she lived in a nursing home. As her reluctant guardian, I had become responsible for her affairs since my father had divorced, then abandoned, his wife of 35 years. Twenty-seven years old, a single parent, living on $325 a month, poverty it seemed had hovered at the borders of my whole life. The good life was missing in action.

Surely my self-proclaimed moral, virtuous, honest, behavior deserved a reward. I was doing everything in my power to make life better. While I completed a bachelor's degree in social work, I was trying to take the 'dys' out of dysfunction through therapy and was keeping my seven-year-old son and me housed and fed even when it meant working two jobs. Where was the emotional support of family and spouse? The good-paying job? When did I get to go to Europe and the Caribbean?

Like most of America, I defined the good life as a high paying job, marriage, 2.5 kids, a great extended family, a house in the suburbs, two cars, a yearly vacation, and good health insurance: externals nowhere to be found in my life. The American Dream I couldn't materialize. A standard which constructed the slide rule by which I factored my life. No wonder the answers were wrong. In retrospect, I laugh. This was not me at all. I loved my independence; one child was plenty; I hated housework; I was a mediocre cook; and I wanted to dedicate my life to making the world a better place—tough to do if you have laundry, grocery shopping, cooking, cleaning, and life planning responsibilities for 4.5 people. Painfully I was hooked, programmed, to want a cultural standard unrelated to who I was.

One day I noticed U.S. Andersen's book *Three Magic Words,* a gift from my sister, lying unread on the bookshelf. Magic, that was what I needed. A blink of an eye, a twitch of the nose and *voilà.* But the magic was not about rituals, incantations, and quick results. It was about changing from within, recognizing ourselves as pure spirit, that We Are God. The idea resonated for me. I turned within, practiced Andersen's meditations faithfully. If I could not achieve the good life by working on the outside, perhaps I could create it from the inside. I changed avenues, but not destinations. My goal was still money, love, travel, peace, everything smooth.

Several years of dedicated practice followed. I changed substantially. My life changed little. I was battered and bruised from imitating a salmon swimming upstream. Sometimes I felt better about my circumstances. Periods of peace occurred. But the good life was a mirage. Innate wonder about the meaning of existence lurked in my psyche and nudged me forward.

Perhaps intellect would provide answers. After twelve credit hours of philosophy, philosophers seemed as clueless as the rest of us. They appeared in possession of great wisdom only because they effectively articulated the questions: was there a God? was there an absolute good? what is the nature of existence?

I refused to swim in the swamp of esoteric questions about the nature of the universe. Centuries have been spent arguing moral and ethical relativism, determinism, teleological and cosmological arguments for the existence of God, the reality of evil, and other obtuse debates. One thing seemed clear: physical existence eliminates certainty and cultivates mystery. We hold beliefs based on our experiences and what we are taught.

I began work on a master's degree in religious studies (Eastern religions). My continuing personal search combined with the knowledge gained from ancient wisdom stirred awareness from deep inner sources. The good life had little to do with outer manifestations. One did not *create* a good life, one *lived it.* "Your duty is to be; and not to be this or that," were words of wisdom from Sri Ramana Maharshi.[1]

I had to give up wanting outer circumstances to be different. As a Buddhist might say, "detach, detach, detach." How did one do that?

> *The way that will relieve your woes on the physical plane will also take you to the highest spiritual realizations. And the way is simple. No resistance.*
> —THADDEUS GOLAS
> THE LAZY MAN S GUIDE TO ENLIGHTENMENT

Ramanuja is supposed to have said: "Let what comes, come; let what goes, go; find out what remains." What remains is the mystery. What remains is All That Is, That I Am, unknowable, indefinable, wondrous, divine.

Again, the mysterious head of a paradox became visible. Having accepted the relativity of good, it was clear it had to be rooted in and blossoming from a set of absolute values. Trying to define a good life from a physical, emotional, or intellectual frame of reference without blending and balancing with a spiritual dimension leads me into, at best, murky water; at worst, the yucky sludge stirred up in the reservoir by bad weather. Good had to grow from my personal experience of communion between my soul and the divine, or I lost my way.

With each step forward, a question answered spawned more questions. What absolute values? By whose determination?

Aristotle's moral virtues—courage, temperance, generosity, philanthropy, pride, friendliness, and justice—are a good, but incomplete, start. What is justice? When am I being friendly? The Middle Way taught by the Buddha leads to peace, insight, and enlightenment. It is the Noble Eightfold Path of right understanding, right thought, right speech, right action, right livelihood, right effort, right mindfulness, and right concentration. But what is right thought? How do I achieve right understanding? What within us motivates moral virtues and right action?

We find our way through the labyrinth of esoteric wisdom and apply it to practical living by turning within, practicing meditation or prayer, and connecting with the divine, whatever we perceive that to be. Meditation is the practice I prefer, albeit a Westernized form: twenty to thirty minutes daily in a comfortable chair with my feet on the floor, my back straight, my hands turned palm upward resting on my legs. No floor-sitting for hours until my legs no longer feel attached to my body. Significant changes–peace, wisdom, knowledge, intuition–have come without the discomforts of traditional meditating form. Even when my discipline wanes and my regularity becomes erratic, positive effects linger.

There is no arguing with results—when I practice meditation regularly my life flows smoothly; I maintain peace and centeredness in the midst of turmoil; I act from a place of love, compassion and a sense of the real me.

Everywhere we turn, rules, regulations, and requirements encase us. But, as Viktor Frankl taught in *Man's Search for Meaning*, even the horrors of a concentration camp do not deprive us of the freedom to decide how we will conduct ourselves within the limitations surrounding us. Freedom is choice, but thought and action cannot be based in ego. Ego-oriented choices are subject to the flaws of human nature. While we rely on ego-based decisions, freedom can run rampant causing havoc and harm.

In the fabric of the good life, freedom is inextricably woven with authenticity and attunement. We must know who we really are, if we are to make choices that constitute a good life. When we live from a genuine awareness of self, our need to act from the ego is lessened. Authentic living comes from realizing our connectedness and living in attunement with the essence that underlies all things. Each supports the others creating an upward spiral leading to more harmony.

And All *includes* me. I haven't won the lotto (yet). My soulmate is living somewhere in Montana (I think). My car is eleven years old and the passenger seat is broken so people have to recline instead of sit if they ride with me. But the good life flourishes in my leased 750-square-foot condominium. The further from the American Dream I find myself, the more a good life envelopes me. I no longer need to hunt it down. In the silence and stillness of meditation, it finds me. The more I connect with my inner being, the more I experience the qualities which, when practiced in thought, word and deed, lead me into the good life, a life lived in freedom, authenticity, and love.

I feel at peace. I do work that feels good. I like myself. I like other people. And if I get angry or upset, depressed, confused, or afraid, I know I have simply lost my way for a moment. I can gaze out my window at the trees, the birds and the beautiful Rocky Mountains. But I no longer look outside for the good life. For that, I look within.

IHLA F. NATION has a master of arts degree in religious studies from the University of Colorado and several years of experience in social services, including working with people with developmental disabilities and placing special-needs children through an adoption agency.

Notes

1. Ram Dass. *Journey of Awakening: A Meditator's Guidebook.* Toronto: Bantam Books, 1978. p.14.
2. U.S. Andersen. *Three Magic Words.* North Hollywood, California: Wilshire Book Company, 1974. p.39.
3. Walpole Rahula. *What the Buddha Taught.* New York: Grove Press, 1974. p. 67.
4. Ibid. p. 69.

DAVID DEBELLIS JONES

Dancing Lights

"YOU AIN'T GONNA MARRY NO SPIC," shouted Bobby Marrone's father as he drank whisky straight from the bottle.

"I love her, Papa," Bobby said, "and she loves me."

Tony Marrone pounded his fist on the table hard enough to rattle the dishes Bobby's mother had brought over from Italy many years before. "You heard me!" he said. "Don't you see her no more."

"Maria Espinosa is a wonderful girl," said Bobby's mother. "Wise beyond her years."

"Who asked you?" Tony snarled with spaghetti in his mouth.

"She is an old soul," Caterina Marrone went on. "One who knows many things without knowing why."

"You don't know nothing!" Tony shouted.

Catarina's eyes dropped to the red-and-white table.

Bobby yelled, "You'd better not lay a hand on Mama."

Bobby surprised himself. Like his mother, he had always cowered before his father's rages, taking beatings in silence. But for the past three years Bobby had worked out after school in Queens at Zeke Miller's gym near Roosevelt Avenue and 92nd Street, where some of the best boxers in the country trained. He had grown from a skinny kid into a muscular athlete.

Tony Marrone rose from the table, eyes smoldering. "How dare you speak that way to your father," he said in a hoarse whisper.

"He didn't mean nothing," Catarina whispered brokenly.

"Shut up, old woman!"

"He's just a boy, Antonio."

Tony jumped up and viciously struck his wife across the face. "I told you to shut up!"

In the past Bobby would have sat there feeling shame and sorrow, but now he stepped forward quickly and punched his father's jaw, with his full weight behind the blow as when he sparred at

Opposite: George Bellows. *Between Rounds No. 1.* Lithograph, 370 × 460 cm., 1916. New Haven, Connecticut: Yale University Art Gallery. Gift of George Hopper Fitch, B.A. 1932, and Mrs. Fitch.

Miller's gym. Tony fell backwards over his chair onto the floor dazed and bleeding. He looked up at his son with fear and disbelief.

Bobby said a silent prayer to the Blessed Virgin for forgiveness as Tony Morrone stood slowly, holding his jaw. "You are no longer my son," he said, his eyes like black coals. "Leave my house. Never come back!"

Bobby went to the hall closet, put on his leather jacket, and returned to the kitchen. His father was wiping blood from his lip.

"If I find out you hit Mama again, I'll come back and make you sorry," Bobby warned his father.

Tony did not reply, but Bobby could tell by his father's fear-filled glance that he would think twice before striking his wife again.

Bobby left the apartment. He walked toward 82nd Street, where Maria lived in a tiny apartment with her parents and five brothers and sisters. It was a cold and windy December night. Snow was falling. He wrapped his scarf tightly around his neck to protect himself from the cold. As he hurried under the El, the ground shook as a train shrieked by. Where would he stay? How would he earn a living? He didn't know. He wasn't sorry he was leaving home. He had wanted to leave for a long time. Now the decision had been made for him. He would not miss his father, but would miss his mother.

She always seemed to be cooking or cleaning or praying, this thin black-haired woman who everyone said he resembled so closely. She rarely smiled, never laughed, her face stayed dark with worry, hurrying everywhere with her short quick steps, to the market or butcher shop or to the delicatessen with her scarf wrapped tightly around her head.

When Maria opened the door, Bobby noticed as he had many times before how much she resembled his mother, slender with black hair and brown eyes. She, too, was serious about life and seldom made light of things. He liked those qualities in her. Unlike the other young men he knew, he did not like women who flirted and giggled and whispered to one another.

He told Maria what had happened as they walked hand in hand along Roosevelt Avenue. "Where will you live, Bobby?" she asked, her eyes wide with concern.

"I don't know. On the street, I suppose."

"No! It's too dangerous."

"Don't worry," he said. "There's an empty warehouse near here. I can sleep there tonight."

Maria shook her head. "I know that place. Drug addicts hang out there. Something awful could happen to you. I'll ask my father if you can stay with us."

"I don't want to impose on your family."

"Please, Bobby, don't let your pride stand in the way of doing what's best for you."

"Don't worry, Maria, I'll find a place."

He let go of her hand. She stood on the sidewalk in the light of a street lamp and watched him go, her eyes glistening. He waved to her until she was swallowed up by the swirling snow.

He walked along Roosevelt Avenue, passing stores secured by high iron gates and dimly lit bars filled with shadowy occupants. He passed a bag lady huddled in a storefront with two blankets wrapped around her and a wino lying on a steam grate clutching a bottle.

When Bobby had first gone to Zeke Miller's gym, he couldn't afford a membership, so he asked Miller if he could earn his dues by sweeping the gym after school. The old man had agreed. At the gym, there was a cot in one of the locker rooms; he wondered if Zeke would let him use it. He couldn't think of anyone else to turn to.

Zeke Miller was in his office when Bobby went into the gym. Bobby told him what had happened at home, then asked if he could sleep on the cot that night. "Use the cot as long as you need to," Zeke said. "I'm just sorry about you and your old man. What're you gonna do for money?"

"I don't know," Bobby said miserably.

"Old man Swenson tells me you do a good job sweeping up," Zeke said. "He's retiring at the end of the week, so I need a janitor. You want the job? It won't pay much, but it's something. You're a smart kid. You'll get a better job in time."

Bobby's eyes lit up. He loved the gym. Working here would allow him to exercise two or three hours a day. Years ago he had learned that while his friends got their highs from crack, marijuana, or alcohol, he got his from exercise. Whether pounding the heavy bag, running on the circular wooden track, sparring in the ring, or swinging up and down on the parallel bars, afterwards he felt like a feather floating on a cloud, his body relaxed, his mind clear, his emotions calm.

Working as a janitor did not pay much, and he barely got by, but Bobby was able to work out as often as he wanted, and he had enough money to rent a cheap room in a rundown rooming house near Roosevelt Avenue. When he wasn't seeing Maria, he spent his time watching boxers work out at the gym. Even though he did not want to become a boxer himself, he loved the sport and liked watching fighters train, especially Chico Calveras, the welterweight champion. The sportswriters called him the best pound-for-pound fighter in the world. The wiry muscular Mexican was quick, agile, and a powerful puncher. However, Calveras made it plain to Bobby one day that he did not like him. Bobby was sweeping the floor when he got in Chico's way as the brooding fighter was leaving the ring after a sparring session.

"Get out of my way, you dumb dago," Calveras snarled. After that, Bobby gave Calveras a wide berth.

The surly boxer was the least of Bobby's worries. What Bobby wanted most was to buy a diamond engagement ring for Maria, but even the least expensive ring cost more than he could save in a year. "Precious stones are a waste of money for those as poor as we are," Maria had told him. "It's our love for each other that counts."

But Bobby was determined to buy her a diamond ring, not only as a token of his love, but because he wanted the world to know that Maria was his girl and off limits to other men. One afternoon as he pummeled the heavy bag in the gym and brooded about how he would get enough money for the ring, someone said, "Hello, kid."

Bobby had been so intent on punishing the bag that he hadn't noticed Emelio Banderas, Calveras's manager, watching him.

"Hello, Mr. Banderas," he said.

"I've been watching you work out, kid. I like what I see. You do good work in the ring, too. You're fast and you're strong. How many fights have you had?"

"None," Bobby said. "I spar with some of the fighters, but only for the exercise. I don't want to be a boxer."

"Even a fool could see that you were born for the ring," was the reply. "And I'm no fool."

"I don't like to hurt people," Bobby countered. "My father is like that. I don't want to be like him."

Banderas laughed. "I like you, kid. If you change your mind, let me know. I'd like to be your manager."

The next day, a commotion broke out near the ring. Bobby was flicking his gloved fists at the light bag, making it go rat-a-tat-a-tat, when he saw Calveras waving his arms wildly.

"I got a fight in two weeks, you jerk," Calveras shouted at his manager. "Get me a sparring partner, or I'll find another manager!"

"If you promise not to half-kill every fighter I bring in," Banderas argued.

Calveras cursed and stalked into the locker room. Banderas was about to follow, but then stopped short, stared at Bobby for several seconds, and came over.

"How would you like to make some money, kid."

"Sparring with Calveras? No way. He'll kill me."

"I'll tell him to take it easy on you."

"He's a mean son of a bitch."

"You go three rounds with him, and there's three hundred bucks in it for you. But you have to go the distance."

Bobby blinked. He could buy an engagement ring for Maria with that much money!

Fifteen minutes later Bobby danced about in the ring as he waited for Calveras to come out of his corner. He said a silent prayer to the Blessed Virgin to keep him from harm as Calveras came rushing at him.

"You're that dago who sweeps up around here," Calveras said. "It pisses me off I got no one to spar with except a loser like you."

Bobby flicked a jab at Calveras' head. The champ dodged the blow easily, saying, "I'm gonna make sliced ravioli out of you, you dumb wop, so my manager gets me a real sparring partner next time."

Calveras let loose with a barrage of lefts and rights that sent Bobby reeling into the ropes. Bobby fought back as best he could, sometimes snapping back Chico's head with a left jab, but he was no match for the champion. He waited for Banderas to shout to his fighter to take it easy, but the older man said nothing.

By the end of the round, Bobby was groggy from head blows. He was bleeding from the nose and winded. He gasped for breath as a cut man dabbed at his cuts and spilled water into his mouth. He sloshed the water around and spit it into a bucket. He didn't want to continue, but Banderas had said he would get no money unless he went three rounds. Bobby made the sign of the cross as he left his corner for the second round.

"Praying ain't gonna do you no good," Calveras smirked. "Nothing can protect you from me." And, sure enough, Calveras' punches seemed to come at him from everywhere at once. Bobby's eyelids were soon nearly swollen shut, his lips bruised and purple, and his ribs red with welts. By ducking, back pedaling, and dodging, he managed to finish the round. As a corner man worked on him, he kept telling himself *only one more round to go.*

As he left his corner for the final round, he said another silent prayer. *Blessed Virgin, protect me, not for my sake but because of Maria and our love for each other.*

Calveras danced out of his corner, a glimmer of hate in his eyes. "Haven't had enough, huh? This round I'm gonna smash your face so bad you won't recognize yourself." He hit Bobby with a straight left that sent him reeling. As Bobby came off the ropes, Calveras sent a looping, overhand right that sent him sprawling to the canvas.

Bobby tried to rise as the referee counted over him. One, two, three . . . Light-headed, he struggled to his feet by the count of nine. He stood with his gloves raised, waiting for the onslaught that was sure to come.

As Calveras came toward him, Bobby became aware of a strange pulsating light hovering near the Mexican's head. The light was as brilliant as the midsummer sun. It was a sparkling, undulating point of light that stayed in constant motion. Sometimes it hovered around Calveras' head; other times it danced close to his body. Bobby didn't know what to make of it until he heard what seemed like a woman's voice whisper in his ear, "Bobby, aim for the light!"

Bobby felt a burst of energy that seemed to come from nowhere. He rushed at Calveras and threw punch after punch at the dancing light. No matter which way his opponent shifted, he was hit by every punch that Bobby threw. Then, as if by magic, the single light changed into three separate lights. No matter which light Bobby aimed at, the blow landed. Bobby hit the champion with upper cuts, left hooks, straight rights, and overhand rights.

Calveras backed away, hurt and desperately trying to defend himself. With 30 seconds left in the round, Bobby hit Calveras flush on the jaw with a vicious right uppercut, and the champion fell to the canvas like a sack of pesos. He lay flat on his back, out cold.

Later, as Bobby took his money from Banderas, he said angrily, "You lied to me. You didn't tell him to take it easy."

Banderas smiled. "I wanted to find out what you were made of, kid," he replied. "I found out."

"I could have been hurt."

"Take it easy," said Banderas with his winning smile, "I'm gonna make you a rich man." Handing Bobby a business card, he added, "Come to my office tomorrow and sign a contract. You're gonna be the next welterweight champ of the world, and I'm gonna be your manager."

Bobby took the card. He didn't especially like Emelio Banderas, but the thought of becoming the next champion of the world appealed to him. He could become famous and wealthy beyond his wildest dreams. Was the purpose of the light to tell him that his destiny was to become a boxing champion? The more he thought about the experience, the more certain he was that he'd received a sign from heaven that he was to be the next boxing legend of the world.

Later that day he went to a jeweler on Roosevelt Avenue and bought the diamond ring. Then he called Maria and asked her if he could take her to dinner. She accepted the offer.

When she opened the door that night, she looked at him with horror. "What . . . what happened to your face?" she said, her right hand grasping the silver cross around her neck.

"I sparred with Chico Calveras, the boxing champion."

"Why did you do such a foolish thing?"

Bobby reached into his coat pocket and took out the diamond ring. "So I could buy you this," he said, slipping the ring on her left index finger.

"It's beautiful," she said, but her smile faded. "I told you once that you didn't have to buy a ring. I meant it. And you certainly shouldn't have gone into the ring with a prize fighter to get it."

"I knocked him out," Bobby said proudly.

"How can that be?" she said, astonished.

Over dinner, he told her everything that had happened. The more he talked, the more excited he became. Barely able to contain himself, he said, "I've been given a sign. God meant me to be the next welterweight champion of the world."

Maria said nothing for a long time, staring silently at her food. "What's the matter?" he asked her at length.

"You *were* given a sign, Bobby, that much is true," she said. "But are you sure you know why your prayer was answered?"

"I just told you why," he said impatiently.

"But you didn't pray to become a boxing champion. When you prayed you said, according to your own words, `Blessed Virgin, protect me, not for my sake but because of Maria and our love for each other.' Am I right?"

"Yeah. So?"

"Your prayer was for our love. It was an unselfish prayer. That's why it was answered."

"Don't you see," he whispered furiously. "This is my chance to be somebody. You and I will have more money than we've ever dreamed of. Tomorrow I'm signing that contract," Bobby said.

"Listen to me carefully, Bobby," Maria said. "Who is the man you despise the most?"

"My father."

"Why do you despise him?"

"Because he is brutal."

"If you became a prize fighter, wouldn't you become the same kind of man as your father? Wouldn't you be hurting others with your fists just as your father has done so often to you and your mother?"

"But, the dancing lights . . . "

"Miracles happen every day, Bobby, but we cannot presume to know the will of God. We must follow our own hearts. This, alone, must be our guide. And you have a gentle heart. Do not go against your own nature."

Bobby stared into his coffee cup for a long time, saying nothing. Then he smiled, reached across the table, and intertwined his fingers with Maria's. "My beautiful Maria," he said. "What would I do without you?"

Maria smiled back, her eyes aglow.

DAVID JONES's short stories and feature articles have appeared in *American Astrology, Chrysalis Reader, Dogwood Tales,* the *Philadelphia Weekly,* and various other literary magazines.

DON EULERT

Playing Alone in Spring

To get a week's work done in a day,
playing alone,
to get a week's work done in a day

First I have to patch the roof groin
first I have to heat the tar
first I have to build a smallish fire

and in every pause look up the hill—
who is coming, through two locked gates?
They could get the greenhouse sides on
we could get the winter garden in

Or else I am lonely, the first
category of my life loneliness . . .

From the fire, tar spreads a dark honey;
this is a roof-pleasure of sealing the house
and looking down at what next to do;

this is the task of seeing the green
mourning and celebrating the solstice,

this is the garden worked alone, this is
the day off to practice for death

to reach five-fingered into the ground
to feel the grain and blossom tempered
in preparation with my hands, they
draw chords from the sun on my back.

The March wind ruffles like a shawl
letting in just enough of the cold.

DON EULERT, professor of cultural psycholgy at California School of
Professional Psychology, San Diego, has published three volumes of poetry
translated from Romanian in addition to four collections of his own work.

JOHN GOLDFINE

First Pressing

IF YOU DRIVE DOWN GOOSE HILL ROAD IN THE FALL, Goose Plantation's last dairy farmer, Winfleet Sharp, will usually be out on one of his three ancient John Deeres, harvesting corn or plowing. He skirts the field edges whenever possible, swings the tractor right out into the field, just the way he does in the spring to avoid the kildeer nests in the new furrows. Of course, the killdeers are gone by October; he's jockeying so as not to crush the apples fallen from the trees along the stone wall.

Dian McCarthy. Pencil, 1997.

Winfleet's grandfather, Levi Sharp, sold the stumpage and when the land was clear, he broke ground. By the third spring of frost heaves, Levi Sharp and his oxen and stone boat had nearly half a mile of stonewalls. One evening in April of that third year, after chores and by moonlight, he and his boy, Orlando, dug a hole alongside the wall, where it met the road, and planted a fork of rootstock. Twenty-five strong paces for the second hole and then twenty-five more for the last.

"What kind of apples are they?"

Levi smiled into the night where Orlando couldn't see and answered with no trace of amusement: "What kind we want. We'll graft in a couple of years." Orlando said nothing. Levi said, "What's your favorite?"

Orlando didn't speak for nearly a minute. "Snow," he said finally. "That'll be our first then."

If you drive down the Goose Hill Road in mid-May across the muddy fields, against the greening woods penned in by stone walls you'll see evenly spaced bursts and sprays and swags of pink-white apple blossom: all Levi Sharp's work, and Orlando's, and Winfleet's too, Orlando's son.

Mike Sharp is partly responsible for a half-dozen or so of the younger trees, but he and Winfleet haven't been out in April evenings, after chores, for at least a dozen years. Mike is twenty now, and he was six or seven when he told Winfleet that he'd miss his TV show if he had to help dig holes. As Winfleet turns the manure spreader at the bottom of the Kildeer Field, he always glances at the last tree he and Mike set out and tells himself that one of these days soon he has to prune it and graft some decent fruit-stock onto this root-run-wild. Winfleet remembers his eighth birthday when he was given a little grafting knife as his present and wonders if Mike still has that good Ka-Bar he bought him years back.

The cider press cost ten dollars and twenty five cents from the 1896 Sears, Roebuck, and Company catalog. A little brass plaque on the screw brace was stamped 'Mt. Gilead.' The antique dealer who comes through every year or two offered Winfleet's wife two-hun-dred-and-fifty, but Winfleet knew it's not replaceable, and he had never yet in his life bought cider.

Not long after the dealer's last visit, his wife showed Winfleet a photograph in *House Beautiful.* A living room in California featured what appeared to be an exact match of the Sears press but all golden with varnish, unlike the press out in the barn. Three spiky plants grew out of the slatted pommy tub.

He said nothing, but his wife teased him anyway. "I'll polish it up and put it right in the middle of the front room."

Like his dad, Winfleet is partial to Snow apples, but no good cider was ever made with a single variety. A mixture of tart and sweet Snows, Roxbury Russets, Winesaps, Spies, even a few crabapples make full cider. When Winfleet was a boy, he and his two sisters, his mother and father, and some of the neighbors all turned out to gath-er windfalls and haul them in behind the team. Nowadays only Winfleet's wife and Mike were around to help with the apples.

Actually, this past five or ten or so years, Winfield has taken an October afternoon and just done it himself, collecting only enough for a dozen gallons, which is all his freezer will keep green. The Sharps never have been drinkers and Winfleet has no intention of ever letting hard cider pass his lips.

This year the bolts holding the screw brace to the cider press's oak frame were working loose, and Winfield backed them out, wedged three headless kitchen matches into each of the four holes, and reset the century-old bolts. If he had time, he told himself, he would disassemble the whole thing.

It would be a lot of work: the careful disassembly; cleaning and polishing all the cast iron and steel parts; yarding some white oak, drying and hauling it to the sawmill. Then he would turn new wood, using the old rotten stuff for a guide. That's how the cider press should be rebuilt—properly. But no dairy farmer in the State of Maine has that sort of time.

Winfleet dumped a half grain-sack of apples into the hopper and figured that he could press four gallons before chores. After the grinder chopped the apples into pommy, Winfield pushed the tub under the screw-driven piston, laid a broken pickax handle into the screwtop, and began to pace around the press, pushing the handle ahead of him, listening to the expressed juice hissing between the slats of the tub.

When the pommy was compressed nearly as far as it could be, there was a sharp cracking noise, and Winfield lurched ahead as the resistance on the pick handle disappeared. He knew instantly that the pressure of the screw had, after a century of service, at last cracked the cast iron piston in the pommy tub. To replace the cast iron he could cobble something up out of wood—six or eight layers of half-inch marine plywood, glued together, and circular-cut to match the piston would most likely do for a year or two.

The cows called, hungry, teats aching for their evening milking, and Winfleet capped the two gallons of cider he had pressed and got ready for chores.

Next morning at seven-thirty, after chores and while Winfleet ate his daily corn flakes, Mike appeared half-awake in the kitchen. He got coffee from the dripper, loaded it with non-dairy creamer and sugar, and sat down at the table across from his father.

Winfleet knew that men who drove snack delivery trucks did not need as much fuel as farmers, but he still thought his son's breakfast awfully poor. Of course, he said nothing about that.

After Mike had nearly finished his first cup, Winfleet said, "How's things going, Mike?"

"Okay."

"We've got some cider in there if you want a thermos today."

"Thanks, Dad. I'll get a soda at one of my stops." Winfleet went back to his corn flakes. After a minute Mike said, "How much did you get this year?"

"Two gallons so far."

Dian McCarthy.
Pencil, 1997.

"Is that all? Didn't we used to get more?"

"Well, yes, we do. The piston split while I was pressing. I'll have to jury-rig something."

"Too bad. Well, I'm out of here. Bye."

Winfleet seldom spoke without thinking, so his next remark surprised him. He knew Mike and knew it was a mistake as soon as it was out of his mouth. He said, "I could use a couple of sheets of half-inch marine plywood. Are you coming by there on your way home?"

Mike said, "Well, it's Friday night. I might not be home 'till late. Where I'm going the stuff would probably get stolen off of my pickup."

Winfleet wanted to know nothing about such places. He looked at Mike and nodded, trying to convey an apology for the original remark. Moving toward the back door, he said, "I better see about replacing the blower in the silo." A moment later, he heard Mike's pickup gathering steam slicing the angle between the drive and the Goose Hill Road.

Winfleet didn't see Mike Saturday morning or Sunday morning either, and only once the following week, but they were both busy men, and this was not unusual. In fact, what with one thing and another, they were able to speak very little over the next month.

Two days before Thanksgiving and Winfleet's wife said to him at the supper table: "Take two gallons of cider out tomorrow and defrost them."

Winfleet said, "I haven't repaired the press yet."

"Is it broken?" Winfleet had always thought it somehow rude to answer the obvious when the other person must surely already regret the question, so he said nothing to his wife.

She said, "We need something to serve Thursday."

Winfleet said, "Yes, but I haven't any cider."

His wife sighed. "Okay, I'll take care of it."

He stood and said, "I guess I'll see about that mastitis."

Thursday Winfleet scrubbed up much earlier than he would have liked, and stood talking to his brother-in-law, thinking about the precarious state of the oldest John Deere's transmission. Before spring he would have to overhaul it completely.

"Let's eat, everyone," his wife said. The family moved, creased and slow, toward the dining room. Winfleet heard his wife say from the kitchen, "Mike, what about those pitchers? Mike?"

Winfleet sat at the head of the table and began work on the turkey. He heard the back door slam.

In the kitchen Mike said, "No problem, where's the pitchers?"

His mom said, "They're out on the table where they're supposed to be. I told you to bring those jugs in here a half-hour ago."

"Okay. Calm down."

"No, don't go in there," Winfleet's wife said. "You act like you were raised in a barn. You can't bring the original container to the table. Bring the pitchers in here."

Mike said, "What's the difference, for godsake?"

Then, from the corner of his eye, Winfleet saw something red move by. Mike said, "Okay, folks, here it is, store-fresh from the grocery. Who wants some cider?" He was holding up a glass gallon jug. On the label was printed 'Bessey's Real Farm Cider' and under the words was an apple the shape of a tomato and the red color of the sweet candy apples at the fair, the red Winfleet had just seen go past. Everyone stopped for a moment and looked at Mike who made the jug gurgle by pivoting his wrist. Two of Mike's little cousins shouted, "Me, me!"

But Mike turned to his father and said, "Dad, you're the cider guy here. You ready?"

Winfleet's two sisters down the table stared at him, and Evie's mouth began forming a question. Winfleet turned from them to his son and nodded. His glass clinked against the jug of cider and clinked again harder as Mike weakened under the weight of it.

From behind Winfleet, his wife said, "Mike, why didn't you put it in the pitchers like I asked you?"

Winfleet lifted his glass and drank. The cider was thin—all "mac," only the one variety. To his wife, he said, "It doesn't matter."

But it does, it does.

JOHN GOLDFINE teaches at Eastern Maine Technical College in Bangor, Maine.

WILLIAM E. MARSH

Wholeness as Holiness

ALTHOUGH HOLINESS IS IN ITS CLASSICAL SENSE THE IDEA of a rigid and uncompromising consecration or setting apart to a higher moral pattern or presence (a good illustration is the way that holiness is presented in the Hebrew and Christian Bibles),[1] it is also a deeply felt state of personal satisfaction, spiritual, moral, or otherwise, in which a person feels at peace (or reconciled) with herself, the world, and the larger forces in her experience. In its ultimate practical form holiness is wholeness, the bedrock on which individual equanimity is constructed and the undergirding from which it moves and functions. It is a liberating state of being that enables its holder to approach and frame the world with wisdom and grace. It is the road to a positive way of living.

Implicit in holiness as wholeness is the notion of a seamlessness, a state of purity or completeness in mind and being that worldly distractions and errant moral perspectives cannot successfully challenge or impinge. It is a seamlessness in which all the things of mind, heart, and body come together, blending and coalescing in a fabric of open-ended contemplation, pursuit, and integration of what is most true.

This undergirding seamlessness in holiness as wholeness is redemptive, that is, it does not confine its holder in a prescriptive rigidity but instead stimulates and nurtures freedom, a freedom from the base and ordinary, a freedom of pattern and process that moves its holder toward a richer moral experience. It is a state of cleansing, a journey of radical reconciliation with significant moral realities. Not intentionally exclusive (the expression of holiness that has spawned countless religious wars and fratricidal disputes), it frees those who

Opposite:
Dian McCarthy.
Ink wash, 1996.

pursue it from the shortcomings of their moral visions and broadens and more fully unifies and explains the human experience with the divine.

Holiness as wholeness and redemptive seamlessness is a metaphor for the path of existential purpose, the way toward personal and corporate spiritual truth. It is a moral state that defines and frames all others. Holiness is the process of all reasonable moral endeavor, the moral journey to a good life, a life that is superior to the experience out of which it comes.

Redemptive holiness is in essence a discipline to achieve a definitive sense of moral understanding and wholeness. It is rooted in a sense of first, the importance of a moral framework (in a redeeming, that is, shaping and nurturing, sense), second, the necessity and challenge of dividing between what is personally important and mundane, and third, the imperative to cultivate through confession and repentance steady progress in the refining of the inner moral being.

Moral frameworks are highly fluid. For example, consider the Buddhist notion of nirvana, in which the adherent finds the fullness of existence (which, paradoxically, is annihilation). Through a complex process of purification, yoga, and meditation, he decisively embraces the impermanence of being and enters into the experience of the unconditioned and nonconstructed, the transcendent in which all things find root. He then finds his life blending together in an integrated whole, an unbroken pattern of non-being that frees him from all metaphysical and material constraint.[2]

The adherent is set apart in a liberating wholeness of mind and body in which he sees and explores the higher patterns of enlightenment in his experience. Moral probity remains, but never in a prescriptive way. It is redemptive, a visionary purity of thought, perspective, and vision. Cleansing of the nonessential as the prelude to entering an ever-higher state of being (that is actually non-being), is prime.

In the same way, the moral frameworks at the center of holiness suggest a state not of blind and unconsidered conformity to an ethical rubric, but an experience of redeeming enlightenment and moral becoming.

The Hebrew notion of *shalom* conveys a state of completeness or soundness permeated by a sense of peace and contentment. The one with *shalom* is at peace with herself and her god; she is reconciled to the various realities and contingencies in her life and feels confident and secure in her place in the world. She has made her peace with the moral patterns, as she sees them, in the universe.[3] Although *shalom* necessarily implies a measure of conformity to a force larger than the human mind, it is in its essence the crown of a redemptive relationship with that force, the expression of a continuing effort to move toward greater enlightenment. *Shalom* is the fruit of a relationship with a moral framework that liberates even as it demands submission, a state of being (and way of life) in which the holder experiences a growing perception of the interconnectedness of all things.

The Islamic doctrine of submission to Allah offers similar benefits. The one who has submitted himself and his life to Allah feels secure in his hands, confident in his ability to shepherd him through his life. He finds his peace in the essential goodness and greatness of Allah's will.[4]

Although *shalom* and submission to Allah point to a holiness that is steeped in the laws of an uncompromising god, they also reflect a state of being conditioned by a conscious choice to move toward a wholeness of thought and perspective. They represent a holiness that affirms a purification and reconciliation with larger moral realities, a holiness as wholeness, a holiness of deep and abiding inner peace. Like the Near Eastern notion of wisdom as behavior that is consistent with the moral order resident in the universe, holiness as wholeness is the adherence to a moral framework consistent with the divine realities one senses in the universe.

Although moral frameworks represent significant decisions to accept some things as useful, good, important, and true, and to reject other things as unnecessary or evil, they are only helpful if they have redeeming personal and social value. Moral frameworks are not so much about doing as they are about being. They are benchmarks as well as experiences, hinges between inner and external peace, healing formulations that are as broad as the cosmos in which they occur.

In holiness as discipline is the essence of dividing the important and mundane. Holiness is the product of a melding of an almost infinite number of life experiences, the fruit of a vast web of journeys, adventures, and insights, all of which each person evaluates and assimilates according to one's perception of moral value. It is the result of carefully analyzing what to retain as well as what to let go, a cautious reflection on the value of each life experience or circumstance. Holiness demands embrace as well as self-abnegation and denial; it involves far more giving up than it does accepting or taking.

Holiness as discipline is the art of discerning between what is really important and what is merely necessary, of mastering a loyalty to transcendent spiritual wholeness amidst a world devoted to the transient and temporary. It is a restorative experience that moves toward a perfection of character.

When a loyal adherent of Tibetan religion nears death, his lama reads to him from the *Bardo Thödol (The Tibetan Book of the Dead)* about the dazzling light he will soon encounter. This light, the lama advises him, is the presence of his own self, which is the ultimate reality. It is the final experience of earthly wholeness.

Even after death, however, the adherent must continue to seek purification. Earthly wholeness is only the beginning of the ever greater experiences of seamlessness which the afterlife will unfold for the one who walks the right way. It is the entry into the richer holiness.[5]

St. John of the Cross, a sixteenth century Catholic mystic, saw life in much the same way. In his *Dark Night of the Soul*, John set forth a complex process by which he believed the religious novitiate enters into the fullness of God. Through meditation, self-denial, and spiritual aridity, the novitiate gradually sheds the extraneous and sinful and passes into an expectant state of rich spiritual open-endedness in which he hears God's voice without darkness or guile. It is a state of numbing and cleansing clarity.[6]

The *Bardo Thödol* and John's dark night of the soul illustrate the essentials of holiness as the dividing between the important and mundane. Both are rooted in a belief in discipline, that holiness as wholeness is a discipline that enables the adherent to travel into the deeper seamlessness that undergirds existence and the larger realities that control it. Moral frameworks define the patterns of wholeness, while discipline describes the processes that contribute to it. Whether discipline is geared toward creating greater visions in the afterlife or shaping the soul in the present, it remains the guiding light of wholeness, the mechanics implicit in the movement toward enlightenment and a good life.

The penitential aspects of holiness represent not so much confession and repentance of wrongdoing to a god as they do a process that identifies and acknowledges attitudes and worldviews that detract or deter from the effort to achieve the reconciliatory and harmonizing experience of which holiness consists.

The Greek word for repentance, *metanoia*, describes a turning around, a turning around from what one was or did and a commitment to pursue a different path. This turning around is total and irrecoverable, a radical changing of one's being. Simply resolving to alter one's actions will not do, for this merely scratches the surface of what needs to change. *Metanoia* is changing the thinking behind actions, a restructuring of the moral fabric that is woven into the soul.[7]

Confession is a way of acknowledging human imperfection. It is an act of humility that enables people to recognize that they are not morally consistent and ethically true. It forces people to admit that regardless of how pure or holy they think they are, they nonetheless tread a very narrow line between wholeness and moral bankruptcy, and spiritual glory and moral shame. Confession is a reminder of human fragility and moral dependency, a telling expression of innate human need.

Confession also underscores the inability of people to change themselves on their own. Although the core of an individual's spiritual experience, that is, the part of the soul from which the profoundest moral judgments are made, is, as William James pointed out many years ago, a unique encounter between the individual and his sense of moral presence that an outsider cannot always readily explain, it is ultimately expressed in the community of which that individual is a part.

For this reason, holiness requires community to explore the practical outworking of its inner meditations. It shines most fully in the culture in which it is experienced and expressed. Though holiness is a spiritual experience unique to the individual, it is challenged, shaped, and expressed within the forces of society. Holiness is an absolute experience in human communities studded with gray.[8] The confession implicit in holiness establishes peace, a kind of *shalom* between person, conscience, and the community of human beings. It affirms and upholds each person's covenant with the human community and the creation of which that community is a part (and on which it is dependent).

For example, in the shamanic healing process among the Yurok Indian tribes of California, the prospective patient must undergo a lengthy cleansing in her community before the shaman will consider seeing her. This insures that the patient is pure and fit, individually and corporately, to stand before the magic and spiritual forces which the shaman will invoke. While the purity is redeeming and is foremost the patient's experience, it also contributes to and reflects the spiritual experience of her tribe.[9]

Greek mythology provides another perspective. Because of the polluting power of homicide, even the Greek god Apollo, after he murdered the Python, had to be purified. Although he expressed his inner picture of right and wrong when he carried out his deed, Apollo also bent the integrity of the universal order on which all beings, including the gods, depended. He purified himself in order to realign his picture of what was holy with the dictums of a broader universal holiness. Even a god couldn't act in moral isolation. Apollo had to recognize that holiness and the moral standards which enter into it was a restorative experience for him as well as the cosmos in which he functioned.[10]

In one of the classic prayers of the ancient near east, the Hittite king Mursili eloquently confessed the nation's wrongdoing in the face of a plague that had decimated the population of the country.

The people believed that the gods would only relent with the punishment that this plague implied if the people repented of their impurities and sin. Corporate wholeness demanded confession of the attitudes and behaviors that had moved the nation away from the singularity of purity it was obligated to honor and pursue.[11]

Community, however, has limitations. Jesus' major complaint against the Pharisees (the religious leaders of his day) was that although they appeared to obey every point of the Jewish law, their obedience was only as valid as the community in which it was exercised. Within their tight and tiny brotherhood, the Pharisees believed they were repentant and pure. Set against the perspective of the person who believed he preached a God who was bigger than all human communities, they were not.[12]

In his *Siddartha,* Hermann Hesse tells the story of a young man who searches for the self that he believes is implicit in what he is (and in what he is to be). After years of looking in many different places and devoting many hours to rigorous repentance and self-discipline, the man finds in a river where he has worked a number of years as a ferryman the redemptive experience for which he longs. In his perception of the river, he decides that his self is in being absent yet present in the unity of all things, in dissolving himself in the eternity of each moment even while he melds himself into all things.[13]

Holiness as wholeness is the same way. Taken as a picture of a good life, a life in which optimism, wisdom, sobriety, and forward movement prevail, holiness as wholeness (individual and corporate) underscores the unity toward which most people strive, the seamlessness and integration of thought and action and environment that forms the goal of much of the human experience. It renders the human experience present even while blending it into the future.

As wholeness, holiness is not confining or prescriptive, but is open-ended. It is to seek purity and interconnectedness through discipline, a discipline in which a person exercises circumspection and repentance to achieve redemptive experiences that bequeath greater personal understanding. Although this effort begins and ends with the individual and her picture of moral realities, it is validated and highlighted in community. Personal holiness is beholden to the environment, the human and animal (and, logically, the divine) communities in which it is formulated. Just as wholeness is unity in the purity and good of all from which it draws its strength, a good life is only good when it implies good for the cultures and worlds of which it is a part. Holiness never occurs in isolation. Its power is in its linkage between the growth of the self and the interplay of that self with the community in which it lives.

A lover of the good life as it unfolds in the immense holiness of each moment, WILLIAM E. MARSH is a writer who holds advanced degrees from Fuller Seminary and the University of Chicago. He lives with his family in Barrington, Illinois.

Notes

1. See especially the laws in the book of Leviticus and how they circumscribe behavior that defers to the holiness of God. Reference as well Moses' encounter with God in Exodus 3 and the way it demonstrates how uncompromising the Israelites believed God's holiness to be. Paul's admonitions to his readers that they are temples of God (1 Cor 6:19) illustrates the Christian perception of the black-and-white character of God's holiness.

2. Eliade, Mircea. *A History of Religious Ideas.* v. 2. Translated by Willard R. Trask. University of Chicago, 1982. pp. 95–106.

3. See Brown, Francis, et al. *A Hebrew and English Lexicon of the Old Testament.* Oxford University, 1907 (reprinted with corrections, 1978), pp. 1022–1024. See also numerous Psalms (34:14, 85:10, 147:14) in which the author talks about finding contentment in God.

4. See *The Koran* (or *Quran*), Surah 3:19, 8:45.

5. Eliade. Op. cit., v. 3. Translated by Alf Hilte-beitel and Diane Apostolos–Cappadona. pp. 278–381.

6. St. John of the Cross. *Dark Night of the Soul.* Translated by E. Allison Peers. New York: Doubleday, 1990.

7. Arndt, William F., and Gingrich, F. Wilbur. *A Greek-English Lexicon of the New Testament and Other Early Christian Literature.* The University of Chicago, 1979. pp. 511–513. See also works by Jim Wallis on structural evil, and effecting personal and corporate change.

8. James, William. *The Varieties of Religious Experience.* New York: Random House, 1929.

9. See *The World Atlas of Divination.* Consulting editor John Matthews. Boston: Little Brown and Company, 1992. pp. 15–16

10. Eliade. Op. cit., pp. 270–271.

11. Gurney, O.R. *The Hittites.* rev. Oxford University, 1961. pp. 165–166. See also the relevant KUB texts.

12. See Matthew 23:14 ff. and parallel texts in Luke and Mark.

13. Hesse, Hermann. *Siddartha.* Translated by Hilda Rosner. New York: New Directions, 1951.

JEAN A. KISER

Things Change

I've never thought
much about the smaller,
probably unimportant
things that change as
one becomes older:
fingernails chip, crack.
Breasts sag, clothes droop.
Hips widen.
The vacuum—stubborn,
difficult—challenges
every corner,
hardly fits in the
suddenly too small
bathroom.
Husband retires,
sleeps late so
silence governs
until mid-morning.
Then he becomes
a shadow in every room.
Money is tight,
fixed, spent too fast.
(unnecessary things
are but a wish)
So you read, write,
dream. A chance you've
never had before.

JEAN A. KISER is a Conncticut writer who has been published in many journals. She co-instructs a writers' group and is active in her local government
as an advocate for wetland and woodland sanctuaries.

THOMAS KRETZ

On
My Own Pond

I dug it for exercise and suntan
after clearing scrub trees of short yearning;
first one to touch their damp earth-clinging roots,
last as well, laying them out to dry for burning;
died resolutely, went quietly as Giordano Bruno
in the foul Roman marketplace of Campo dei Fiori,
spiked iron gag so as not to ruin the Sanctus
of the Vatican Boys Choir not to change voice,
hear the loud snaps and crackles of bone.

Fish and friends wiggle in safety;
I never intended the hole *per se* as hole
or to preach a new doctrine of salvation,
diverting the crooked stream to fill it,
an act Susquehanna braves would never dare,
afraid the angry Manatou might kill it,
though they would dance to the stake
knowing that even mature men are children
with a strong song in their moan.

THOMAS KRETZ is currently the business manager of the Jesuit Historical Institute in Rome where he is also researching and writing a history of the Jesuit Brothers, because, he says, "enough has been written about the priests."

PERRY S. MARTIN, EDITOR

Sky Meadow Tales

Marcia Gaiter.
The City of the Head.
Oil on masonite,
48 × 35^{15}/$_{16}$ inches,
1954. Collection
of The University
of Arizona Museum
of Art, Tucson.
Museum Purchase.

The following stories were written by participants in a workshop on Experiencing the Feminine of the Divine, led by the Rev. Dr. Dorothea Harvey at Sky Meadow at the Temenos Retreat Center in West Chester, Pennsylvania. As a way to experience the goodness of one's own feminine, each person wrote a life fairy tale. When life's complexities were simplified by the imagination, each writer discovered an inner truth.

The Girl Giant

ONCE UPON A TIME there was a little girl who knew that a giant lived inside her—a really big woman giant! "Now who has ever heard of a woman giant?" she would say to herself. Most of the fairy tale books she had read contained wonderful pictures of looming, large male giants, good ones and bad ones too. The little girl never told a single person about her woman giant because she was afraid, not exactly of the giant, but of what her giant would do once she was set free. She was also afraid that people would laugh at her and say that she just imagined all this nonsense.

So the little girl lived a long, long time with her giant locked behind the bars of her bones and muscles, organs and blood. Meanwhile the woman giant on the inside grew and grew and grew. In time she was taking up so much space that the little girl knew she would have to burst open soon or die from having her insides crushed. She felt very frightened indeed.

The day of freedom came at the perfect moment. The child had arrived at the place of terror: she was face to face, toe to toe, with a purple-black mountain higher than anything she could ever climb or cross. She stood like a dwarf with the dark, immovable hard mass blocking her path. For a moment she was breathless and thought she would faint or fall down. She turned around, thinking she could run away, and maybe find a safe place to just lie down—or even to die.

What she saw as she turned to run was the huge mountain that she had already climbed without really ever knowing she was climbing all the while. All around her were mountains growing grey and distant as they stretched their heavy heads toward the sky.

"Let me out!" shouted her woman giant in a great big voice. Her voice was so loud that the little girl covered her ears with her hands. But the voice would not quiet down or soften. "Let me out, now!" the giant shouted. The little girl was shocked because, until this moment, the voice of her giant had always been a still, quiet voice—a voice that made her feel safe and good on the inside.

"Let me out now, or you will die!" the giant's voice insisted even louder than before. This was a deadly, serious moment for the little girl. There was no other way to go, nothing else remaining for her to do, so the little girl opened her arms, her heart, her organs, her bones, her blood, her head. As she let go of everything, an absolutely magnificent female giant grew from her insides out. She grew and grew and grew as if being spilled out of an endless birthing well. She grew larger than all the immovable mountains. She grew fair and strong and beautiful, and she shook out her long, black hair against the wind and blue of the forever sky.

Suddenly the giant looked down to where the amazed, speechless and delighted child stood. She bent ever so slightly and gently to pick the child up and cupped her carefully in the palm of her soft hand. Then putting her hand over her heart, the giant stood tall and straight again, and lightly lifting her pale blue skirt, she stepped easily over every mountain and danced a kind of happy step. The child leaned into the heartbeat of the giant's warm breast where she heard and felt the rhythm and pulse of all creation's inner core.

—BERNARDINE ABBOTT

Everything Right

ONCE UPON A TIME in a far away place a long, long time ago, there lived a little girl. She was a very little girl, and she lived in a house with a cold, sad mother and a warm, imaginative father, and a very good big brother and a very bad big sister. Everybody was big, and she was small. She was afraid.

She was tongue-tied, so when she tried to talk, everybody laughed.

She wanted to know why things were the way they were, but when she asked questions, everybody laughed.

Or else her father got mad and yelled, and she didn't know why.

When she played with her brother, her sister would come, and they would run away from her. She couldn't run as fast as they could, so she cried and everybody laughed.

She thought if I can Do Everything Right nobody will laugh at me.

If I Never Cry nobody will tease me and call me a baby.

And to Never Cry and Do Everything Right I have to Know Everything.

So she did.

She was a very good girl who did Everything Right. She went to school and was the smartest kid so she could know everything.

And she Never Cried.

But she was very lonely.

So she got married to Live Happily Ever After.

But she discovered When She Did Everything Right and Never Cried she was still lonely.

So she had babies. Six of them. And she discovered that when you have six children you can't Know Everything, Do Everything Right, and at least Not Feel Like Crying.

One day her children all grew up and went out into the world to seek their fortunes. So she went out for a walk in the forest. She felt the pine needles under her feet. She saw new leaves growing on the trees. She saw flowers blooming. She saw golden water flowing in the river. She saw the sun set and the full moon rise.

She found elves and fairies and dwarves and giants and all sorts of people in a big circle. And they said,

"Come and play with us. And if you don't Do Everything Right, we will hold your hand. And if you Don't Know Everything, we will dance with you. And if you fall down You Can Cry, and we will hold you."

She looked at them and said "Really? I don't have to Do Everything Right? I don't have to Know Everything? and If I hurt I Can Cry? Really?"

They altogether said, "Really, because we love you just the way you are." She took off her shoes and held out her hands and said, "Let's dance."

—PERRY MARTIN

Blue Eyes

A BLUE-EYED BOY LIVED in a cottage in the deep woods. The big brown-eyed people said "You are not like us. You must work. Blue eyes can't be trusted." The blue-eyed boy called himself a "blue." He didn't know what a boy was, but he knew there were blues and browns and blues work, and can't be trusted.

The blue-eyed boy grew, and gathered and hunted in the woods to feed the others back at the cottage. One day he sat in a clearing to look at the trees doing their work. Someone else walked into the clearing. This someone looked very much like the blue-eyed boy. That someone's eyes were very much the same—the same color. "Hello," said the blue-eyed boy. "You are a blue-eyed boy like me. Who do you work for?"

The other laughed, and sounded quite different from the blue-eyed boy.

"What is blue?" asked the other; "I've never heard of that. Oh, and I'm not a boy. I'm a girl."

"You don't know what blue is?" asked the boy. "How do you know who is good, and brown-eyed, so you can do as they say? And what is a girl? I've never heard of that!"

They stared at each other. Each saw clearly that the other had no idea what is important.

"You work for people?" asked the girl. "Are they your parents?"

"Parents—I don't know what that is, either," said the blue-eyed boy.

The girl looked at him. "You are a slave," she said. "Someone stole you, and you don't remember. Walk out with me. They can't do anything outside their woods. Out here we live with families."

"Tell me about families," said the blue-eyed boy.

The girl explained that people have mothers and fathers and how babies grow and become mothers and fathers. She pointed to things in the woods and showed how the earth and sky come together and make life.

The blue-eyed boy was scared, because once one of the brown-eyes said "father" and another said that was a bad word. Once the blue-eyed boy got angry and shouted 'father' and the brown-eyes beat him for that. So when the blue-eyed girl told him that he was a boy, and would become a father, he felt strange. She told him he had a mother and father and could find out about them at a great palace where all the records were kept. That seemed even more strange. He felt scared and lonely because now something was missing.

They went to the palace and found the records for the blue-eyed boy. Indeed, he had a family once, and every one thought they all had died in a fire. How he had fallen into the clutches of the brown-eyes no one knew.

The boy and the girl led a party of helpers back to the great forest to visit the brown-eyes and explain that they couldn't have slaves any more.

Arriving at the place where the cottage was, they found no one, and no sign that anyone had ever lived there. The blue-eyed boy wondered if he had made it all up. The others said, "That's all right. This has happened before."

They returned home, leaving the boy and the girl there. They sat and watched the trees do their work. And then they began building a new place to live. They live there now, between the earth and sky, with the trees, and their blue-eyed children.

—MICHAEL DAVID

Water World

ONCE UPON A TIME there was a little girl named Dorothea. She lived in a big forest where there was always fog, so you couldn't see the real shapes of the trees, just sort of know they were there. She was very carefully carrying a basin of water, walking *very* carefully, so she wouldn't spill any because if she spilled any the whole place would dissolve, and there wouldn't be *anything*—and she wouldn't survive. In the fog she could sometimes see a dim shape of her mother and father back behind the trees somewhere. But if she spilled any, *everything* would dissolve and she wouldn't *be.*

One day she saw another little girl also carrying a basin of water very carefully, and she said to herself, there are other people like me. She smiled at the other little girl, and the other little girl smiled back. She knew the other little girl was as scared as she was, and that if *she* didn't do something, the other little girl would just be gone. And she realized she was sad and lonely, and that she had to say something. Nothing in the forest could be as bad as loneliness, so she got very brave and she said, "Hello."

Then the other little girl said "Hello" back. And something was different.

And she said to the other little girl. "Let's stop carrying this water so carefully. Let's *spill* some."

So they did, and the whole world did *not* dissolve, and instead there was some light and color that came into the forest, and they could see real tree shapes and real ground with grass that you could tell how far it went. And they felt *good* about themselves and what they had done, and still the ground did not dissolve. And they spilled more water, and they ran and played and didn't care what spilled, and more light and more color came into the world, and so did parrots and monkeys and elephants and all kinds of animals you could see. And the little girl said, "I'm glad I met you, and I'm glad we are friends, and I want to see you some more, and I *know* I like knowing you, and it feels good to me. I'm still a little scared about what may happen, but I know it is okay to feel what I feel, and that is good, and we are okay, no matter what we feel, and we can say it, and the sun is *shining*, and we can *see* it.

—DOROTHEA HARVEY

PART IV

Nothing Wasted

Everything, but everything, needed to equip my new abode flew to me from nowhere and everywhere without asking. One day my attention was drawn to two armchairs I had acquired. They sat opposite each other in front of the fireplace. Was I getting ready to return to work? The next day on a walk down Commercial Street a young man rolled out of the Foc'sle Bar and pleaded with me to help him with his life. He became my first appointment after a self-imposed eight-year sabbatical. He came. He sat in one of the armchairs. I sat in the other.

SWEDENBORG'S PARADIGM OF THE GOOD LIFE ends with the stage symbolized by the Sabbath, when "God saw everything that he had made, and behold, it was very good . . . and he rested." He gave this stage the same name as the process of getting to it: *Becoming New.*

As the heading of this page suggests, the transformation into newness incorporates and fulfills all the living that preceded it. As the acorn is present in the whole oak tree, and the caterpillar in the chrysalis shimmers in the wings of the butterfly, all our trials and dreams, successes and failures live in the new being that grows out of making do with what we get.

But where beginning required searching, and changing ourselves required work, becoming new is an effortless transformation that is seldom noticed by those who experience it, except in retrospect. Swedenborg calls it a gift from God, a gift that is given only after we have tried to change ourselves (which, of course, we have no power to do). By divine alchemy our feeble but persistent effort is transmuted into a transforming power, and we become what we turned toward and worked for.

Stannard, Eller, Smith, and Mills describe lives that muddled through uncertainty, confidence, joy, and pain to (or approaching) a fulfillment never envisioned during the process; and Hitchcock helps explain how that happens.

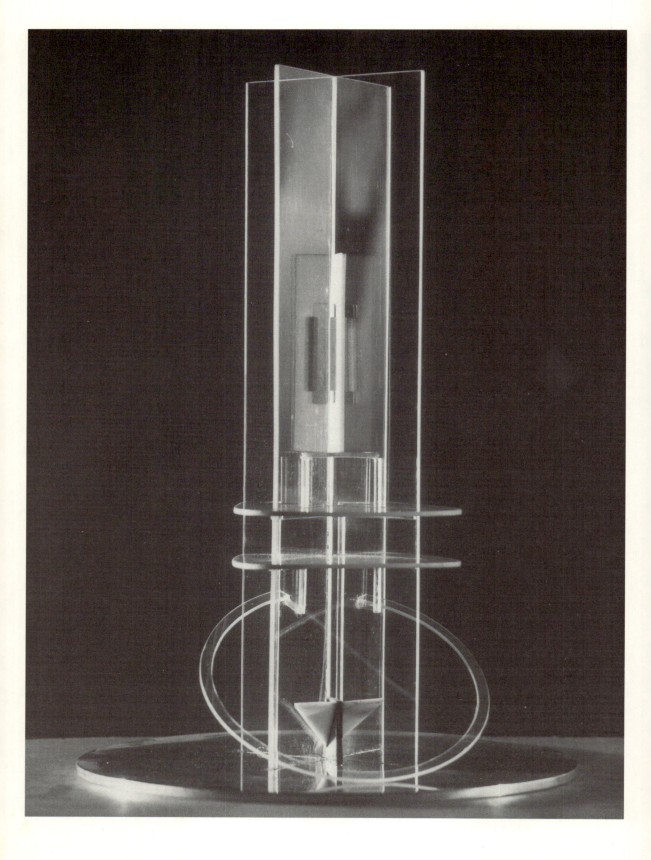

KATHERINE STANNARD

Nothing Wasted

Alchemical Order

Everyone's spiritual search in mature life is for what Jung terms individuation (undividedness), development of the whole person, integrating all the functions and hidden pieces of the unconscious with consciousness.

IN 1975 I BECAME a licensed lay reader and eucharist minister for St. Luke's Episcopal Church in a small Massachusetts community. During the preceding decades I had sampled a theological smorgasbord: infant Episcopalian, preschool Unity student, school age Methodist, Baptist, Christian Scientist, Roman Catholic (following the lead of my childhood friends), high school returned-Episcopalian (St. John's and St. Paul's Cathedral in Vermont), young adult and bride at Emmanuel Church in Boston, newly married at All Saints' in Worcester (with an occasional turn at St. Paul's Cathedral, the Roman Catholic diocesan center of Worcester), and finally, in 1949, settling into St. Luke's in Worcester, convenient to our new home in the suburbs, where I have worshiped ever since. During that same period my professional career had careened wildly from librarian to art teacher to learning disabilities tutor. A final turn at graduate school had landed me as a professor in the psychology department at Framingham State College in Massachusetts. But by 1985 my college teaching had tended to become routine, and my restless spirit began a search for something more.

So I began studies with Education for Ministry, a theological course for lay people, which opened spiritual doors I never knew were there, and laid the foundation for my writing. Through this course I also discovered Jung, who was *persona non grata* in my psy-

Opposite: Nahum Gabo. *Column* formerly *Model for Glass Fountain,* ca. 1928, rebuilt 1938. New Haven, Connecticut: Yale University Art Gallery. Gift of The Société Anonyme.

chology department but who immediately appealed to me. Like Jung, I had searched for God with various earnest groups both in and out of church settings. That search now included early Gnostic beliefs as I explored Jung's analytical psychology. Jung also asserted that the center of each human psyche held the God image, the closest we can know in this life. For a Christian, this image has the face of Jesus. For a Moslem, Allah is approached through the Koran. For the Native American, God is the Great Spirit, known through manifestations of the natural world. For any faith, the divine can be revealed in unique ways, suitable to circumstance and culture.

Within our spiritual search for individuation, and in our unconscious, dwells the personal shadow, not necessarily dark and evil, but simply unknown and unaccepted. In many cases personalities of others that trouble us are demonstrating aspects of one's own shadow. When we come to see this, we also begin to better appreciate others in their personal spiritual journeys. So individuation is also opening the heart to the divine, which is holiness, wholeness, healing.

For Jung, dreams frequently describe the condition of what is unknown in one's psyche, what is going on in the unconscious. Early in my study of Jung I had what he would have termed "a big dream," in which my dream self was finding great difficulty in accomplishing what appeared a simple task. Before me stood a wooden spindle, about four feet high, beside a pile of white starched cloth squares with a hole in each center. My job was to fit these on the spindle, smoothing them out so they would lie flat. But it was not easy, for one corner of each square was gathered up resembling the corner of a fitted bed sheet. No square would lie flat, but persisted in bunching up at that one corner. Upon awakening I puzzled over this, and continued to puzzle, but today, some eight years later, believe I can understand the message.

At the time of my dream I did not know very much about Jung's types. He had described two polar positions for each of two mental functions: perception (sensing/intuiting) and decision-making (thinking/feeling). (Feeling is coming to a conclusion on the basis of values, and does not mean emotions. The other aspects have usual definitions.) It was later that I learned that my inferior function (closest to the unconscious and likely to be troublesome) was "thinking." So my unconscious logical processes were tangled up and would cause me trouble when I tried to develop balance among the four functions. I couldn't get all four parts of the white squares even. Although I had managed to accomplish research projects and to direct students in their own, I didn't enjoy hypothesis testing and statistical analysis. My thinking was to be sorely tested in 1991.

Study of Jung rejuvenated my work as a teacher and I now dis-covered I could write about subjects that interested more people than just me. Some new being seemed struggling to emerge as part of my life. I recall speaking to my class one morning about transitions, re-assuring them that they were not married to their major, there would be opportunities for new ventures. I rather worked myself into a pas-sion on this subject, exclaiming that "right now I feel like a chrysalis—something new is trying to emerge." A day or two later I found in my mailbox a sample copy of *Chrysalis*, with encourage-ment to correspond with the editor concerning manuscript submis-sion. So the new creature became, at least in part, a writer and a pub-lished author. I had finally integrated my undergraduate English mi-nor with my enthusiasm for art history and Jungian psychology.

I thus began to receive invitations to speak to various psycholo-gy organizations, particularly about psychology and art. One orga-nization emphasized Freudian interpretations of art; creation was al-lied to madness. I was not persuaded. Rather I saw the painters striv-ing to express their wholeness in their work, and often archetypal symbols pervaded paintings made in later life, which I interpreted as an artist's spiritual journey toward personal individuation. My ar-chetypal white squares were my first remembered intimations of my own potential for wholeness.

I also explored Swedenborg's writings, finding what I read not incompatible with my own intuitions. The New Jerusalem provides a destiny for my elfin soul. Visions of heaven and hell provide guide-posts for my own earthly journey. And heaven, as an experience of useful action, ever deeper spiritual growth, is most attractive to one in increasing years. How wonderful to continue the good works that are imperfect in the world, into their perfection in the next.

Accumulated years give perspective on changes, people, events. Retirement provides time to reflect. Where did the time go? What did we learn? In 1990 those questions arose from my own shadowy depths and demanded consideration. And, what about my inner life? My psyche seems to me wiser but not older. My spirit doesn't age but only changes. And, what is the destiny of my spirit, psyche, soul—this inner living person? These terms for inner experience may be synonymous, but they vary in connotation. And, how is my every-day experience connected to this inner life?

To write about inner development, I struggled with terminolo-gy. I finally surrendered to Thomas Moore's description of "soul" as a "dimension of experiencing life and ourselves."[1] I also found help in Jung's words about the soul. "Soul is the living thing in man, that which lives of itself and causes life. . . . Were it not for the leaping and twinkling of the soul, man would rot away in his greatest passion, idleness. . . . But to have soul is the whole venture of life, for soul is the life-giving daemon who plays his elfin game above and below human existence. . . . Heaven and hell are the fates meted out to the soul and not to civilized man, who in his nakedness and timidity would have no idea what to do with himself in a heavenly Jerusalem."[2] So this elfin, living daemon doesn't age but only carries us toward a world of wonders. My own inner history comprises search and return, and begins with a myth.

A Family Myth

MY BLACK IRISH HAIR AND EYES are apparently from encounters between Irish colleens and seamen from the Spanish Armada. My maternal grandmother was born in County Galway, where, over the centuries, the Malavels became respectable, a fine family of boys and girls. Then came tragedy. Great-grandmother Malavel died, leaving great-grandfather with the children. It seems that fathers were not trusted with children and one day the local parish priest came to great-grandfather's house and announced that the children were to go to a family where there was female presence. Now, great-grandfather was a churchman, but one with an Irish temper. He became enraged, picked up a stick, and beat up the priest. That is why I, an only child, was born and baptized a Protestant.

Examination of my personal history reveals some elements of my slightly giddy personal pattern in which I begin to intuit the opportunistic action of divine order, surprises that await an open heart, and a repeating theme: my personal varieties of religious experience. Occasionally I feel like an ecumenical movement all by myself.

My experience of God's divine order always lies at the center. For instance, during the Great Depression our food ran low. "We don't have anything for lunch," my mother said. I guess I was inventive at that age. "Don't worry," I reassured her. "I'll make lunch. Just don't watch." In preceding years my mother had spent many hours canning fruit and jelly. There were some prunes and syrup left in a jar. I found remains of grape jelly and some pieces of bread. I remember spreading jelly on the bread, putting the prunes in sauce dishes, and, for a beverage, diluted the prune syrup with water. "Lunch is ready!" My parents came to the table, looked at my inventions and cried.

During World War II, when it became apparent that my sick father could no longer work, I left school and, as a confirmed liberal artsy young woman, found work as a technician amid world renowned scientists at the Radiation Laboratory at the Massachusetts Institute of Technology. After the war, in an absolutely loony senior year scholastic move I had to transfer to a Boston area college, where I also had to compete with returning undergraduate veterans. I finessed this obstruction by entering Boston University's graduate school, taking courses in art history to put aside until I earned my bachelor of arts degree.

When a new bride and new to Worcester, I was hired as an assistant librarian at the Public Library where I was very much second string, since I was informed that "my credentials were inadequate." Nevertheless, this second string position opened doors to a profound spiritual experience. Some of my duties required answering questions at the service desk, where I met a cross-section of Worcester County. Remember, I was twenty-four years old, and still blooming. One young man hung around a lot, making me quite nervous. Somehow we got into conversation, something about patriotism. He was avidly reading in the religion section, and declared with conviction that "nation is second to God." His earnestness impressed me, and I thought over his remark. Shortly after this encounter I was reading C. S. Lewis's *Problem of Pain*, and was so struck by the author's description of God's descent into human form (as if a human being were to become "a slug or a crab"), that I fell momentarily into some kind of spiritual darkness. When I emerged, my surroundings had changed. My body felt uncommonly weightless. When I saw some of the unlovely library patrons—who then, as now, often came in only to find a warm chair—they and all other people seemed to shine. Never again have I been blessed with such an epiphany, but never have I forgotten my vision of what I believe the world is really like. Thanks to the provocative words of that unknown young man and my reading, I realized that when God takes first place among allegiances, other relations take on their divine order and life is aglow with love. When I review my personal story, His order shines through apparently random occurrences.

Variety Show

MY FATHER WAS SON OF A FRENCH-CANADIAN LUMBER MAN who, when he came to Vermont, attended the Congregational Church. In both my parents there was a considerable strain of English heritage, which probably mediated some of the tensions of my forebears. So I was baptized in Erie, Pennsylvania, as an Episcopalian, which meant little to me as a child.

My mother's good friend who lived near us when I was four years old was a Unity student. A great convenience was her six-year-old daughter's consistent attendance at Unity Sunday School and the invitation to me to come along. That was where, as I sat among my circle of friends and waited to listen to God, I learned to meditate. We were instructed to sit with hands palms up, and wait in silence, an unfailing way to centering, calm, and an expectation that I could hear God's voice in my heart. This expectation has renewed itself in various unexpected ways in later life.

My mother became a faithful reader of Unity literature. We had a nice house, a 1928 Overland, and, in 1929, enough to eat. But in 1930 we were confronted by the terrors of the Great Depression. When we drove into Erie, I saw long gray lines of men waiting for charity meals. Ice cream cones were five cents. One day, when shopping, my mother acceded to my impulsive request: "Give me a nickel!" I grabbed the coin and ran to a little girl about my age and put it in her hand. I think it was my last act of giving money as a child: my father lost his job at the General Electric Company and our family was humiliated into welfare. But we still had a place to live.

As the Depression deepened, we had a little cardboard Unity Prosperity Bank in the kitchen and Silent Unity supported our family with its prayers. My mother cried easily in those days. She had married security with my father and lived it in our house; now all her hopes were threatened. One spring day in 1932 my Uncle John drove up in his Buick. His face was pale and he called to my father. "Bert, you have to get out. The bank is foreclosing on your house. They'll take everything—furniture, your car, everything!" I have a freeze-frame memory of my father standing paralyzed while my mother wailed. We packed everything our car would hold, and (how I don't remember) got our furniture into a truck. So we lost our four-year-old suburban home and fled in the night to Vermont, to the family of my unemployed father. We hoped to receive our willed share of my grandfather's estate, but family tensions obstructed the legal process. Vermont in those days was not a welcoming place for poor refugees. Meanwhile, I attended the Congregational Church, whose Sunday school education comprised brightly colored little leaflets of Bible stories. I liked to sit close to my teacher because when she wasn't looking I could rub my fingers against her soft Hudson seal fur coat. At the Congregational Church at age nine, I was served a small cube of soft white bread and a thimbleful of grape juice at Communion. With no liturgical sense, I felt merely fed, and during the Depression that was good.

From grades four to eight my school friends changed, so did my church-going. I bent like a birch tree, accommodating myself to the faith of my friends: Methodist, Baptist, Roman Catholic, Christian Science—I think that covers almost every church in town.

Already my elfin inner-life confirmed Jung's description of the soul as "butterfly" reeling drunkenly from flower to flower and living on honey and love.[3] As I reflect on my ecclesiastical tastings, I see it as preparation for my later open heart—a willingness to see God in many guises, to hear His voice in words spoken by human beings, to know Him as expressed in community and love.

The large white Congregational church dominated the center of the village, near the library and Music Hall, across the street from the public school. But behind the school was a little gray stone church that appeared closed, and consequently remained a mystery to me in my ecumenical adventures.

Back to the Future

ENTRANCE INTO HIGH SCHOOL WAS A GREAT EVENT. The first floor of the school housed grades 1 through 8. To attend high school, we went upstairs. But there was more: young people came from surrounding hamlets, from one-room schools, to gather in our central community, a whole new mix of people, potential friends, and adventure.

Mary was one of these friends. "Were you baptized?" she inquired. "Oh, yes. When I was a baby." "Into the Congregational Church?" "No. We lived in Erie then. (Pause) Mom! What church was I baptized in?" From a distance: "The Episcopal Church, when you were a baby." "So," said Mary, "How come you go to the Congregational Church?" "Because my aunt is organist." She truly was, but I think my congregational faithfulness was mostly inertia. "It's time you were confirmed," Mary declared. "I'm going to be." This had rapidly become a confusing state of affairs. My inquiries resulted in several clarifications: the little gray church was an Episcopal mission; Mary and her family always went to the little church on Sunday evening (!) for Evening Prayer since that was their turn for work from the harried vicar; confirmation meant "really joining the church" as an adult; Mary's mother would give me confirmation instruction.

All this sounded fine to me. I would get to see inside the only unknown church in town. The liturgical beauty appealed to me as (I so believed) a budding artist. I could also sleep on Sunday mornings. I would be a member of the Young People's Fellowship, and as such, would travel to other Episcopal churches, Mary's mother serving as chauffeur. And in the YPF, I could meet more boys! I really liked the Episcopal church!

Then I made an astonishing discovery. In those dear dim days, religion had not been banned from public discourse. We prayed in school. We recited the Lord's Prayer, and, at least in some grades, we listened to a psalm (usually Psalm 1). In high school there was more. We had religious education conducted by the clergy of our preferred church. It was then that I was told that "yes, we were Protestant

Episcopalians, but better yet, we were really Anglo-Catholics." And our rector was "Father!" This was heady stuff! I belonged to the Bridge Church. Ours was the church that was destined to gather all under her generous wings, and all the churches I ever attended would be one, and I had been on the right track all the time. Of course, I eventually learned that "all may be one" but not necessarily Episcopal Anglo–Catholic ones. But I would certainly be ready for any re-unions.

So began my life as a reconstituted Episcopalian.

High Church and Higher Education

MY COLLEGE DAYS began at the University of Vermont as an elementary education major, a choice that required no tuition, but the expectation that I would teach school in Vermont. I wanted to be an art major, but art was not part of the program, and if it were, the money wasn't available. I also discovered the possibilities of graduate degrees and at age sixteen set my heart on a doctorate and college teaching.

Mary and I had entered college together, but in the press of new friends and studies, our ways parted. I discovered the Canterbury Club, a higher version of the YPF . Now I attended a cathedral! At Rock Point Conference Center, I discovered that we not only had "fathers" but also bishops, monks, and nuns. Truly, the Episcopal Church appeared to cover everything clerical.

College courses were entertaining, and I made sure that I got all the liberal arts courses that I could fit in my schedule. Life was easy. My family had moved to Burlington, we had built a new house, and life was good. Then my father was transferred to Boston, and we kept two households. That was manageable until December 7, 1941, when my father came home very ill. He recovered from surgery, but we decided that life was too important to live apart, so we moved to Arlington, Massachusetts, and enjoyed the summer of 1942. In 1944 my father died; my mother had to go to work and I postponed my junior year while continuing to work at the Radiation Lab. By age 19 I was forced into maturity, and my spiritual beliefs were sorely tested. St. John's Church, which offered support and Father Hatch, helped us keep going on.

Some gleams pierced my dark. I met my future husband George at MIT where he was a young engineer just out of college. As our relationship grew, he became more anxious, for my name was French, and in his experience, that meant Roman Catholic. He, too, was an only child. How relieved he and his family were when they learned that I was, as were they—an Episcopalian. Life became easier, but then the Laboratory closed; World War II was won.

With help from scholarships, a full-time job, and greater maturity, I returned to the University of Vermont, this time as a French major. But at the end of a year, I had to return to my ill mother and evening courses at Boston University. Nevertheless, I felt at home with charismatic professors and part-time jobs. One of these was at Boston's Emmanuel Church where I got paid for teaching Sunday school. Those Episcopalians were not poor.

Despite my complicated schedule, I continued being a member of St. John's Canterbury Club and trusted the future. I think God's divine order arranged my curriculum, for in 1948 I received both my bachelor's and master's degrees. And I also married the Episcopalian engineer, in the chapel of Emmanuel Church.

At Home and Work

MARRIED LIFE STARTED in a furnished three-room apartment with shared bath (we never met our fellow bathers). While George became a professor at Worcester Polytechnic Institute (or WPI, to initiates), I languished at home. Nobody wanted my art history. But the public library needed a person in the humanities division. Not to work with art books. No. The Division Head had that pleasure.

Now in non-ecumenical 1948 Worcester, Roman Catholics had just formed their own diocese with their own bishop and had almost nothing to do with things Protestant. So then I knew why the library wanted me. It was my job to review and order all the Protestant books. That year the World Council of Churches set the ecumenical framework for today's generous attitudes, and I got to order that report. I also discovered the riches of religious writing, especially the work of C. S. Lewis. His clear logic and vivid imagery captured me; I read everything he had written, including his scholarly works. All Saints' Church was near our apartment, and I attended faithfully, often alone.

All Saints was one block from St. Paul's Roman Catholic Cathedral. One of my Roman Catholic co-workers of about my age was as curious as I about various manifestations of Christianity. We adopted the practice of frequently taking our lunch hours to visit one of our churches when there were no services. We prayed together in the crypt of St. Paul's or in All Saints' tiny chapel. I believe that my friend was a little out of bounds in a Protestant church, and I wondered at her courage in taking these ecumenical steps.

A Family

AFTER A YEAR OF MARRIAGE, we decided that my mother was too lonely in Arlington and needed to be with us. We made appropriate financial agreements, and in 1949 she joined us in our new house and family worship at St. Luke's Church. I continued working and my mother liked keeping house, a neat arrangement for me. I moved to teaching art in the public schools, enjoying my work, colleagues, and comfortable house.

My mother and I were often the church-goers. The professor worked six days a week and graded papers on Sunday. I also learned to drive: a 1938 DeSoto. The beginning of trouble. If I had a license, I could drive to church myself. I just had to get the car out of the garage. I almost made it. The crunch of bumper on garage door frame got George out of bed, dressed, and in church faster than at any time in his life. "It's cheaper to go to church," he said, "than to re-build the house." George went on to serve St. Luke's in almost every orderly capacity.

By the age of thirty I began to be interested in motherhood, recognizing the maturation of my physical body and conventional expectations of the 1950s. That interest eventually became a passion, and a thwarted longing. I needed to experience more of my "life-giving daemon," a new dimension of expansion of soul. I passed agonizing birthdays thirty-one and thirty-two, and finally realized that my children were coming from an adoption service. So we waited, and waited some more. The more we waited, the more I wanted someone to call me "Mama." After rejections and delays, we brought home our first child, a four-and-one-half month old boy with black hair and eyes to match. Of course, in 1957 one did not work if one became a mother, so I left my current job as elementary art supervisor in a nearby town, and stayed home to learn motherhood. Our daughter arrived from the same source two years later, and, as she became vocal and mobile, she struggled to catch up with her brother. War was declared. Remember, George and I were both only children. I had absolutely no idea of sibling skirmishes, and tried, eventually, to ignore them. My mother, however, watched the children closely, and when some action looked dangerous, would ask, "Do you want him/her to do that?" *Me, sotto voce:* "Of course not, but now I have to do something about it." Our five-member family stayed on a relatively even keel thanks to massive amounts of repression on everyone's part.

So we lived fifteen years as a three-generation family. During that time I continued to practice some kind of systematic private devotions, finding in the silence the same reassuring presence I had met as a pre-school child, and centering my soul in a warmth that thawed

my sometimes chilly interactions. Then, as later, I found myself back-
ing into a divinely ordered event with occasional surprising outcomes. I recognized that God is an opportunist, and opening one's
heart to Him creates a life full of surprises.

During one of these silences, for example, I received an urgent
"pray for Africa." "What?" But in 1962, as now, Africa needed prayers
as colonies struggled with problems of independence. So I obeyed.
Sometime later I was visited by WPI's Protestant chaplain who was
accompanied by two very tall mahogany men, one a WPI student and
the other director of the African Student Service. They had gotten
my name as president of the WPI women's club, which had been true
in 1958 but was no longer. Our home thus became a refuge for young
Africans (mostly Kenyan Mau-Maus) in varieties of Presbyterian,
Roman Catholic, Animist, and Episcopalian. I found them summer
jobs and housing and I also got in trouble over the one Episcopalian.
The African ambassador to the United Nations declared that he knew
I wasn't intentionally "disturbing the harmonious relations between
our two nations." This was true; I simply knew nothing about visas.
The young man got to stay here anyway, and the Episcopal Bishop of
Buffalo took him in.

St. Luke's supported us through all the milestones of our lives:
the arrival of our first two children, the deaths of our three remaining parents, arrival of our third child, confirmations, adolescent
crises, and all the turns that life makes in decades of family events.
After the dislocations experienced during the Great Depression, I
found security in the rhythms of the church year and the kindness
of an understanding clergy.

My career had turned from art teacher to mother, then to graduate student (again), and to a doctoral program. Finally I became a
professor in the psychology department at Framingham State
College, which I was to enjoy for seventeen years. My love affair with
Piaget's logical theories and Skinner's persuasive behaviorism di-
verted me from my spiritual commitments. Realization of my 35-
year-old dream was exciting and I enjoyed my students. However, after ten years, I realized the aridity of cognitive and behavioral psychology. I needed something deeper and warmer, which I now can
see as God's continuing call, helping me to become what He designed
me to be.

After some years in this relatively conventional path (with some
excursions into New Age activities and transpersonal psychology en-
couraged by a colleague), a WPI faculty member introduced my husband to some varieties of esoteric thinking and soon we found ourselves members of a small fraternal body. Back to meditation in a
group. One member remarked how much Unity's little booklet *Daily*

Word helped her through the tough places of a difficult life. She gave me some copies, and I remembered how my mother had depended on these short comforting words to help her through our Depression difficulties. I got my own subscription, and as I read these messages, I felt at home again. Unity encourages its students to go to any church, and I found that my experience with their writings helped me become a more devoted Episcopalian.

Unity has a beloved Prayer for Protection, calling on the power, light, and love of God which in my own life have protected me from rigidity. Never have I believed that I possess the only truth. I am also protected by my provisionalism! I realized this when confronted by painfully limited Episcopalian religious convictions, once at a workshop and again at an Episcopal social gathering. I was amazed at my revulsion of the expressed dogmatic declarations. (Surely my Hindu friend knows salvation as well as any Christian!) I guess I have been vaccinated against prejudice. And fortunately St. Luke's rector declared himself for universal salvation. How can we limit the eternity of God with our own temporal convictions?

Professor Emerita

WHAT NEW IDENTITY EMERGES WITH RETIREMENT? Certainly nothing I ever expected or consciously prepared for. When I took on a volunteer position of resource development for a nonprofit agency, I soon found that I must develop my logic, intellectual tidiness, and accurate arithmetic, revisiting repressed research methods from graduate school. To raise funds to help rescue disadvantaged children (consistent with my preferred feeling function), I had to integrate my less-developed psychological abilities, all those shadowy aspects that had remained at a kind of toddler stage of development, particularly my logical thinking—another step toward wholeness, another piece of my interior God-image. When pressed for auction materials for fund-raising events, my dormant love of painting awoke in abstract watercolors. People bought them! So half a century fell away as I found another piece of a slumbering psyche.

I find many circular patterns in both my worldly and inner life. It appears that all has been planted for later harvest: creation in art and language, my varieties of school experiences, return to my earliest spiritual learning, return to my liturgical origins, all harmonizing through discoveries, adventures and major life changes into a developing transcendent self.

When questioned some time ago concerning "the real storyline" of my inner history, my best reply was attention to God's voice in my life and my opportunities to respond. I wondered when I would find

my real storyline among the many varied bits of personal history re-
counted here. In fact, this essay languished for some months while I
sought its basic meaning.

THIS DRY PERIOD contributed to more depth in my daemon: soul-
searching in a maze. Sometimes I doubted that I would find an answer, but my daemon persisted with his questions, willing to wait for
a solution. As in so many events in my past, help came from God
through one of His creatures.

St. Luke's has a new rector, Father David, whose energies and
messages have initiated a rebirth in our congregation. His sermons
have always spoken to my own needs. Recently David spoke of "purity of heart." Purity, he said, is not innocence but, quoting
Kierkegaard, is "willing one thing." We in these days struggle with
fragmentation in our lives. How can we hope to live in a single way?
For us, that single thing is to see God amidst our fragmentations, for
truly He is in all His creation and in every circumstance. A search for
such purity, I believe, is my real storyline.

All my past fragmentations of searches and returns have not
been wasted, for in their depths I seem to have been living toward
one purpose. I now have a consistent theme against which to judge
my experience and reactions. My life events have composted into a
rich unique soil from which new growth will always occur. Spiritual
experience reveals an alchemical order: philosophical gold—single-
ness, purity of heart—will appear from silent work within the spiritual crucible of the most common life experiences. In this open-
ended process of transformation with greater security in my purpose, I will continue to find new revelations, new relationships, new
adventures.

Confronted by a life summary at the Biblical three-score-years-
and-ten, I realize that my search has not been only from my human
point of view. The search is reciprocal. God is seeking out His creatures and in His divine order, seeker and sought will ultimately find
union.

Notes

1. Thomas Moore. *Care of the Soul.* New York: Harper & Collins, 1992. p. 8.
2. C. G. Jung. *The Archetypes and the Collective Unconscious.* Princeton University Press /
    Bollingen Paperback, 1980. pp. 26–27.
3. Ibid., p. 26.

KATHERINE STANNARD continues her spiritual journey in a small
Massachusetts community, where she prepares funding proposals, coordi-
nates fund-raising events, and enjoys gardening, writing, painting, life with
her family and within St. Luke's Episcopal Church.

ERROL MILLER

Coming Home

I saw you in Mississippi
among the white frame houses,
quiet country backyards, simple truths.

 You are in all things, you know.

And you were in the rain
that followed me home to Louisiana,
that pounded on your door as I did
upon my arrival from a trip
of too much wanting,
longing.

ERROL MILLER, whose work appeared from time to time in *Chrysalis: Journal of the Swedenborg Foundation*, has recently been published in *American Poetry Review, Maryland Review, Wallace Stevens Journal, Centennial Review, Seattle Review, Roanoke Review*, and other journals. Several new collections of Miller's poetry are forthcoming: *Forever Beyond Us, Downward Glide, Blue Atlantis*, and *This Side of Chicago*.

JOHN L. HITCHCOCK

Forgiving
the Universe

If everything in and around us is indeed moving toward a great union by love, the world should seemingly be bathed in joy . . . On the contrary, I answer. It is just such a world that is the most natural and necessary seat of suffering. Nothing is more beatific than union attained; nothing more laborious than the pursuit of union. —PIERRE TEILHARD DE CHARDIN[1]

Adolph Gottlieb.
The Seer. Oil on canvas,
59³/4 × 71⁵/8 inches,
1950. Washington, D.C.:
The Phillips Collection.

THE WORLD IS NOT AN EASY PLACE for those who *feel the pain of human being* (a sensitivity to the lives of others) and the *pain of being human* (felt from within). Teilhard gives three causes for this suffering. The first is our lack of belonging in a world of differences, or, as he puts it, "unions missed, broken unions, incomplete unions." The second reason for the pain is:

> In order to unify in ourselves or unite with others, we must change, renounce, give ourselves; and this violence to ourselves partakes of pain . . . Every advance in personalization must be paid for: so much union, so much suffering.[2]

The third cause, Teilhard calls the "pain of metamorphosis," *symbolized* by death and dying, but actually *lived* in the process of our own self-development:

> No physical agent can grow indefinitely without reaching the phase of a change of state. . . . On reaching a certain limit of concentration, the personal elements find themselves faced with a threshold to be crossed before they can enter the sphere of action of a center of a higher order. It is not only necessary for them at that moment to rouse themselves from the inertia which tends to immobilize them. The moment has come also for them to surrender to a transformation which appears to take from them all that they have already acquired. *They can grow no greater without changing.* . . . Deaths, death, are no more than critical points on the road to union.[3]

Teilhard is not speaking of physical deaths, but of all those psychological deaths to which we are subject along the road to wholeness of mind, body, and spirit. If we fail to see the necessity of this process of change, our hearts will likely turn instead toward anger at the pain and frustration we feel because of our resistance to that change.

WHEN SOMEONE DIES AN APPARENTLY NEEDLESS DEATH, we tend to say that the ways of God are inscrutable. In fact, we are avoiding an admission that the universe does not make mistakes. We say that "God's infinite wisdom" chose this time and manner of death, but we cannot grasp that process with our mortal minds. This belief in God's infinite wisdom seems humble in the face of divine mystery, but this belief is also an act of turning away from the *saving* process of seeing and understanding universal truths, which are not so distant. But grasping them involves our breaking down the walls with which we protect our unconsciousness. These barriers are the deaths whose meaning, if we had courage enough to look at them, would indeed transform our lives. The deaths that do not force us to revise our understanding of reality are not the meaningful events that transform us or evolve consciousness.

Change meets with resistance and with myriad rationalizations as to why not to change. Self-arguments and anger gather strength, which can only be resolved in a state of forgiveness: the need to forgive and to be forgiven. We can forgive God when we realize the ultimate goodness of nature, and we are forgiven when we move on and into harmony with that divine nature. Both aspects of forgiveness require the courage to see the meaning of intimate deaths and that we face the fragmentation of our own lives.

FORGIVING THE UNIVERSE IS A PRIMARY ACT in sacrificing ego-control, called by Erich Neumann *centroversion,* for it permits us to feel more deeply and to let the Center of centers grasp our being. In defining centroversion, Neumann shows that he is speaking of the same general process as Teilhard:

> Centroversion is the innate tendency of a whole to create unity within its parts and to synthesize their differences in unified systems.[4]

It is painful to perceive our partialness, limitations, and inner moral conflicts. But what Neumann makes clearer than does Teilhard is that the very process of ego-formation—which on one hand makes choice possible and on the other hand clouds our perception of more subtle realities—is part of centroversion from the beginning:

> The tendency of an ego conciousness that is becoming aware of itself, the tendency of all self-consciousness, all reflection, to see itself as in a mirror, which is a necessary and essential feature [of the process]. Self-formation and self-realization begin in earnest when human consciousness develops into self-consciousness. Self-reflection is as characteristic of the pubertal phase of humanity as it is of the pubertal phase of the individual.[5]

Thus, through self-reflection, the perceiving ego participates, or can participate, in its own process of unification. Unification takes place because of our ability, freedom, and need to see and resolve our inner contradictions. But along with the ability of unification, comes the freedom and responsibility to fail *on our own.* We must forgive ourselves for failing and forgive the universe for allowing us the freedom of choice to fail on our own. When we forgive the universe, we really are becoming one with it, and we are also forgiving ourselves for our protracted apostasy.

By insisting on a conventionally "good" God, we ignore self-reflection, contradictions, and the painful realization that life is not perfect. Our blinded faith prevents our healing. You cannot be healed if your suffering is always replaced by the courage not to feel the pain.

Healing is the most profound fact of being alive, and woundedness makes healing visible. Only obstacles develop our creativity, and the ultimate obstacle is our mortality, which is also at the root of our experience of fullness and depth of being. We must forgive the universe for death, both universally and personally, for it pushes us to *live*.

THERE IS NO CONCEPT OF TRULY LIVING that will square with a "fair" universe. While it is true that we all need to learn to live with each other, we are also enjoined by creation to follow our individual destinies. With openness to each other, our differences *might* engender less conflict than they do, but our differences are not the true source of the "unfairness" of the cosmos. Rather the source is the very limitation of each individual view of the world, and yet at the same time the essential need for those multiple individual views. That is, the perception of unfairness is a *mis*perception because it is an individual perception taken out of the context of a more universal view. In our lives and in the lives of others the opposites of God become visible. As J. Robert Oppenheimer put it:

> It turned out to be impossible . . . for me to live with anybody else, without understanding that what I saw was only one part of the truth . . . and in an attempt to break out and be a reasonable man, I had to realize that my own worries about what I did were valid and were important, but that they were not the whole story, that there must be a complementary way of looking at them, because other people did not see them as I did. And I needed what they saw, needed them.[6]

Forgiving the universe is accepting our finitude and partialness, but it is also seeing ourselves as part of the whole, as one of many *needed* parts.

JOHN L. HITCHCOCK, a physicist–astronomer who works in the field of science and religion, is the author of *Atoms, Snowflakes & God: The Convergence of Science and Religion* (Quest Books 1986), and *The Web of the Universe: Jung, the New Physics, and Human Spirituality* (Paulist Press 1991). The latter is part of the Paulist Press series, *Jung and Spirituality*. His third book, *The New Labyrinth: Images of Spirituality from Chaos Theory*, is under consideration for publication.

Notes

1. Pierre Teilhard de Chardin. *Human Energy.* New York: Harcourt Brace Jovanovich, 1969. pp. 84–85.
2. Ibid., p. 87.
3. Ibid., pp. 87–88.
4. Erich Neumann. *The Origin and History of Consciousness.* New York: Pantheon Books, 1954. p. 286.
5. Ibid., p. 89.
6. Peter Goodchild. *J. Robert Oppenheimer: Shatterer of Worlds.* Boston: Houghton Mifflin, 1981. p. 278.

DAVID B. ELLER

Tending the Garden

Who loves a garden still his Eden keeps,
Perennial pleasures plants, and wholesome harvests reaps.

—A. BRONSON ALCOTT, 1868

Heinrich Otto (American). *Fraktur Motifs.* Pen and watercolor, 13 1/8 × 16 1/2 inches, late eighteenth century. New York: The Metropolitan Museum of Art. Gift of Edgar William and Bernice Chrysler Garbisch, 1966. 66.242.1

MY FATHER WAS A GARDENER AND ORCHARD GROWER, a tiller of the soil. His boyhood home, as well as mine, was in the Roanoke Valley of southwest Virginia, amid the rhododendron-covered Blue Ridge Mountains. Our family lived, farmed, and tended orchards for several generations in the small community of Oak Grove on the sun-warmed slopes of Sugar Loaf and Long Ridge mountains. The old 'homeplace' was a four-hundred acre farm where my father, his father, and his grandfather were born, raised, and worked the fields and orchards. To a young boy, everything about the homeplace seemed tired and worn—from the stone springhouse and whitewashed corncrib to the family cemetery and cool root cellar under the main house.

Our ancestors were German–American subsistence farmers who had settled on this land in the 1790s. As far back as anyone has traced, they were "Dunkers," members of the German Baptist Brethren Church (today Church of the Brethren), whose name reflects their manner of immersion baptism. In the nineteenth and early twentieth centuries, Brethren viewed themselves as nonconforming Christians, living separate from the world. To outsiders they were known for their piety, plain dress, prosperous farms, and honesty, as well as for their refusal to swear oaths, serve on juries, or perform military service.

My great-grandfather, a farmer–preacher, was the first to turn part of our land into commercial orchards. To avoid conscription into the Confederate Army, he was forced to flee north (to Ohio) during the War of the Rebellion, leaving behind a wife and four young children. When the war was over, he returned to Virginia discovering that his home had been destroyed and the fields lay fallow. His wife had died of cholera in 1865 and the children had been placed in the homes of relatives. Great-grandfather rounded up his children, remarried, began a new family, rebuilt the farm, and expanded the fruit orchards. His son, my grandfather, continued to expand the orchards and experimented with raising other cash crops such as tomatoes and watermelons. Grandpa was also a farmer–preacher and built the Oak Grove Brethren Meetinghouse with timber from our land.

Tending the earth and religion were thus an inseparable part of my father's heritage. The annual rituals of gardening were an important part of our family's economic and social life. I doubt if my parents thought about whether or not we would have a garden: gardening was simply an accepted part of our way of life. They discussed over supper which hybrid seed corn or variety of tomatoes to buy, various methods of insect control, how much of any crop Mom would need for canning or freezing, and chore assignments for my siblings and myself. The garden and our small orchard always produced more fruits and vegetables than we could use, so much of the produce was given away to needy neighbors and church families.

Early in the spring when there was still a danger of frost, Dad would often prepare a small hothouse perhaps five-by-eight feet, about twenty inches high, with southern exposure, consisting of a framed plot, and covered by two old and well-worn paned-glass windows hinged on opposite sides to the frame. When the windows were closed, the sun heated the soil and air, allowing Dad to force-start tender plants. He would carefully arrange sets of onions, lettuce, radishes, carrots, and tomato seedlings for later transplanting. It was a poor year when the hothouse did not have fresh garden greens before Memorial Day. After a long winter, tasting Mom's first salad with homemade dressing was an exquisite experience that could not be duplicated with store-bought produce.

Our garden was a familiar place, yet finding potatoes beneath its folds was mysterious and the way summer squash grew overnight was magical. The one-third-acre plot was located on a gentle slope between a small barn on the east, a ten-acre peach and apple orchard on the west. To the north was a pasture and woodlot, and up the slope, close to the county road, was my home, which was a converted turn-of-the century negro schoolhouse. A permanent berry patch, perennials such as rhubarb and asparagus, and wild mint for summer iced tea flourished in unity.

Preparing the main garden for planting was great fun because my uncle, who lived a half mile away at the homeplace, would drive the old Caterpillar tractor and plow. The children were usually allowed to ride on the tractor as the field was turned over after its winter's rest; I think he wanted our extra weight. The plow was followed by disking and a cultivator to break up the soil, but we didn't enjoy it when he hooked the Caterpillar up to the county's oldest manure spreader to fertilize the field. When I was older, my uncle retired from tending the orchards and we bought a second-hand garden tiller. Its constant vibration made working the ground a tiresome task.

The ground prepared, I walked behind my Dad as he laid out several rows of sweet corn with a corn planter and sowed beans and peas by hand. As I helped with the planting, the reddish-brown limestone soil felt cool and rich beneath my bare feet and toes, although large clods of dirt and stones were frequent obstacles. My younger brother and I delighted in finding earthworms or interesting insects in the ground, capturing some to tease our sisters with.

Tobacco products were forbidden in our home, but after the corn matured, my brother and I would sneak off and secretly remove some of the dried corn silk. We rolled it up in a curly dry rhododendron leaf or packed it in a homemade corncob pipe, lit it up, and smoked ourselves sick. Once, when Dad was in the garden harvesting beets for pickling, he noticed a strange odor coming from the barn and discovered our mischief; he saw to it that we weeded the corn patch a second time that week.

Dad was proud of his garden. He worked in grandpa's orchards through World War II, then decided not to join his brothers in continuing the family business. Dad found employment as an electrician in a nearby town, but after a day's work he would spend an hour during many summer evenings hoeing, fertilizing, thinning, watering, and otherwise caring for our vegetable patch and fruit trees. It required considerable planning, effort, and labor, yet I don't think Dad necessarily thought of it as work. Yet to our young eyes, if it was play, it was mighty serious play.

For several summers many neighboring communities—through the 4-H and county agricultural extension agent—competed in gardening contests. The competition was usually stiff, but Dad's prize tomatoes deserved recognition. In his later years, a thick-sliced beefsteak tomato sandwich on wheat bread with lettuce and mayonnaise was still his favorite. I am still partial to the low-acid yellow tomatoes, some of which Dad used to save every year for seed.

In addition to producing a glorious bounty, the garden was a great teacher for Dad. To him it was no divine accident that the biblical story of human creation took place in a garden. There was a sacred life rhythm to be honored in the cycle of planting, tending, harvesting, and resting. My brother, sisters, and I received careful instruction on how to plant and cultivate and store up, with the lesson that growing some of our own food gave us a sense of being at one with nature and God. He talked to us more than once about the miracle of how a dormant seed becomes germinated when planted and with proper care the young seedling becomes a mature plant that yields useful fruit. Sadly, at the time, many of these lessons went in one ear and out the other. Only much later did I discover and take to heart Voltaire's advice at the conclusion of *Candide* that, after all else has failed, we should cultivate our gardens.

One crop we could rely on even though I never really knew why we grew them were the gourds. The vines began to climb up the white trellis on the edge of the garden in July and by late August or early September the gourds were fully grown. Usually there were several varieties in many colors, shapes, and sizes. My favorite was beige and resembled a large hook-necked squash, except that the surface was smooth to the touch and often shiny. By late September the gourds had been collected and were stored to dry on newspapers on the back porch.

Late one summer when I was about nine or ten, we were called to a nearby farm two miles up the road. An elderly couple lived there, the husband a second cousin of my grandfather. We knew this family well. They were "Old Order Dunkers," members of a branch of our church that still retained some of the plain Dutch folkways of our ancestors, including distinctive dress similar to that of some Mennonites and Amish. A string of gourds had been used to grace the kitchen door frame and in the fall this kitchen always smelled of apples, cinnamon, and other spices. One of the gourds on the door, the color of eggshells, attracted my attention because of its unusual pointed shape. It reminded me of a star. While pondering the connection between stars and gourds, I first experienced the death of someone I knew and loved.

Lots of people were present that day, and the conversation was quiet. We learned the details of how these neighbors had been in a tragic car accident at a railroad crossing and had died on the way to the county hospital. This family and some of their adult children who lived close by, operated a large truck garden and regularly sold their produce at the farmer's market in Roanoke. Nevertheless, my parents took the family a meal with fresh vegetables and a berry pie from our garden, an offering from our soul.

Dad's soul needed tending, too, and he changed vocations in mid-life. Four of his five brothers, following the example of their father and grandfather, became ordained ministers. So perhaps it was not unusual that Dad, too, felt the call of the set-apart pastoral ministry. During his youth, the Brethren in our area were in transition from the plural, free (nonsalaried) ministry to professional, salaried pastors. Dad had been an active lay leader and chorister/choir director in a few area churches; but after the requisite study and training, we moved when I was sixteen, to his first pastorate in Idaho.

That move was terribly difficult for our family. The Virginia hills and our family's homeplace were filled with generations of memories. My older sister had recently married and was staying behind. My brother and I were not excited about the prospect of becoming preacher's kids. It was June when we arrived at our new home and one of the first things Dad did was to lay out a sizable vegetable garden at the rear of the parsonage. He quickly learned irrigation techniques for the grey volcanic ash soil from the farmers in the congregation and by the end of August he had the finest garden in town. Dad later served churches in California and then went back to southeast Virginia. Wherever he moved in his ministry, he always planted a garden, cultivated fruit trees, and planted native Virginia dogwood.

All but two of the seven churches he pastored were in rural communities where agriculture was still a primary economic activity. Many of his sermons were filled with illustrations drawn from tending orchards, helping with farm chores, or gardening. One of his favorite illustrations was taken from John's gospel where Jesus talked about pruning the vines. Dad knew a lot about pruning and how the process produces better fruit.

One year he gave each of us a Georgia Belle peach tree in the orchard next to the garden for us to tend. We were allowed to sell the crop (a few bushels) for spending money. He showed us how to spray for insects, how to prune, and one summer day, when the peaches were about the size of a large gumball, he announced it was time for thinning. A woman from Roanoke was visiting in our home at the time and walked with us the short distance to the children's grove. Showing off, I climbed my tree (rather than using a ladder), and knocked off the excess fruit. Our guest was moved to tears at seeing the quantity of small green fruit fall, fully covering the ground, seemingly wasted. Only with thinning, however, could the remaining fruit grow larger, mature, and ripen. Dad likened pruning and thinning to discipline and sacrifice in the Christian life; it was good for us, he said, and good for the church as well.

During a visit to my home in his later years, he got it into his head that a huge, difficult-to-reach branch from a tall oak tree needed to be removed so that it would not brush up against the roof of my house. After he had mentioned this problem perhaps two or three times, I told him not to worry about it—we would have a tree company come and prune it away later, in the fall. But this did not satisfy him. Late one afternoon I returned home from the office and soon noticed that the branch had mysteriously disappeared. When I asked him about it, he professed complete innocence and with a twinkle in his eye said that he knew nothing about it. Dad could also be playful when trying to make a point. I have yet to discover exactly how he managed to saw it off, or where he put it.

When I was a student in theological school, I once asked Dad to tell me his favorite book in the Bible. He replied without hesitation, James. Thinking that he would name Matthew or one of the gospels, this answer came as something of a surprise. But Dad thought James contained all the essentials for a devout life, only without a lot of wordy theology. It contained five brief chapters that people who worked the soil could relate to and understand. The religion of James was simple, practical, direct, and integrated into the whole of life. Religion for Dad was like that. It was not something done or talked about only on Sundays. It was integrated into the very fabric of his being. It could not be separated from how he lived or spent his time throughout the week. His gardening, his care and stewardship of the earth, expressed his faith.

Gardening continued to be one of Dad's favorite pastimes, although in retirement, the size of the plot and the number of fruit trees gradually dwindled. I looked forward to visiting him with my family so that my children could experience their grandpa as a gardener. They probably didn't sense the beauty and mystery of his ability to grow things, for this was an insight I myself did not appreciate until years later. It takes a certain amount of life experience to understand the value that comes from performing chores, or to discern how gardening for Dad was a form of release, perhaps therapy, that kept him connected to the important things in life. In his last years, when ill health confined him to the house and prevented him from gardening, he instructed grandchildren on how to plant tomatoes in pots. These pots were then placed on the porch so that he could tend them. He was a gardener until the end, a wise man close to his faith, close to his roots, close to the soil he loved. He was one of those simple saints who tended his garden well, and whose understanding and appreciation of the divine in nature touched all those who knew him.

DAVID B. ELLER is an ordained minister, former executive director of the Swedenborg Foundation and publisher of Chrysalis Books. He is currently professor of history and religious studies at Elizabethtown College in Lancaster County, Pennsylvania.

NAOMI G. SMITH

Sylvia

Sueo Serisawa. *Bouquet*. Oil on canvas, 20×24 inches, 1951. Tempe: Arizona State University Art Museum. Gift of Oliver B. James.

SYLVIA CAME TO THE BACK DOOR AND ASKED IF I HAD SOME LEMONS.

"I don't have any lemons," I said. "Are you cooking something that has to have them?"

She laughed. Sylvia had a low laugh that came easily. Many of her sentences began with that laugh of hers. "I'm making lemon meringue pie," she said.

"No problem. I have a package of lemon-pie filling you can have."

"Oh no," she said. "I'll wait until Duncan comes home so I can go get more lemons."

Incredulous, I asked if she intended to make her lemon meringue pie from scratch.

"Oh yes, I always do."

I watched her trudge back across the yard and shook my head

I watched her trudge back across the yard and shook my head with amused annoyance. Two small children, another on the way, and she couldn't use store-bought lemon-pie filling.

During the time when Sylvia and Duncan were next-door neighbors, another child appeared every couple of years. They moved to a larger house a short way around the circular road where we lived— and more children came. Even though our church community had a tradition of large families, there were those who looked in dismay at their expanding family.

When I dropped by the new house, I often found Sylvia with a bushel of fresh picked fruit, making applesauce or canning peaches. She didn't just cook for her growing brood. Sylvia and Duncan invited the old, the lonely middle-aged, the young adults of the community, as well as their own age group to dinner, for a barbecue, or to one of their parties.

Their life wasn't all parties, charitable deeds, and well-behaved children. Simply because of the size of the family, the usual traumas of child raising were multiplied exponentially. There were the usual and sometimes unusual illnesses, escapades, and hair-raising episodes times six, times seven, and then, times eight. One of the ways Sylvia coped was by being selective about how she expended her energies. Though she cleaned house regularly, a tidy house wasn't a high priority, perhaps because it never seemed to stay picked up for more than half an hour. When you came for a visit, if you had to step over the detritus of a multi-child home, Sylvia didn't apologize, she just ignored it and expected her caller to do so too.

There were indications of the pressures she encountered daily. For all the time I knew her, Sylvia struggled unsuccessfully with her weight, and her fingernails were bitten to the quick, betraying stresses she wasn't willing to talk about, at least not to casual friends.

Though she and Duncan seemed to make it a point of honor not to ask for help, sometimes it was impossible not to. There was the day Sylvia called to ask if I'd drive her to the hospital; she was in labor, hadn't a car, and hadn't been able to reach Duncan at the landscape nursery where he worked.

I picked her up and drove my blue Mustang to the hospital as fast as I dared, chatting about inconsequential things and trying not to panic. Occasionally Sylvia lapsed into silence. I looked over anxiously when she didn't respond to my chatter and saw her frowning, as though concentrating on something in the far distance.

"Sylvia?" I said tentatively. "Sylvia, are you all right?"

A few moments later she relaxed and nodded, and I exhaled as deeply as she and continued my nervous babble.

The nurse who pushed Sylvia's wheelchair down the hospital hallway broke into a run before she reached the elevators. Carl, their fifth son and sixth child, was born twenty minutes later while I waited in the "fathers' room." After about ten minutes more Duncan appeared. Hardly waiting to be told about his new son, he lunged past the nurse and through the recovery room doors. Oblivious of his muddy boots and work-stained clothes, he marched to Sylvia's bedside, folded her in his arms, and kissed her. No one who watched, doctor or nurse, asked him to leave.

They had some tough times. When Duncan was laid off from his job, he didn't hang around wondering where the next paycheck would come from; he started his own landscaping business. Sylvia took over the accounting and office work.

Like everyone else I wondered how she was going to be able to fit in this task with everything else she had to do, but I soon realized that she truly enjoyed this new demand on her energies. She was good at it and loved the challenge.

When news of Sylvia's tenth pregnancy made the rounds, there were those who shook their head in disbelief. But, when the baby was born, the whole community rejoiced to learn that Venita, surrounded by all those brothers, now had a sister.

It was about six years after this, when Sylvia was in her early forties, that she learned she had cancer. Like the rest of her friends, I was shocked at the horror, the unfairness of it. Like many of our church community, I sent over meals, sorted unending loads of laundry, and on occasion cleaned the house while Sylvia had a chemo session. Sylvia approached the fact of her illness as she did everything in her life, with determination and without complaint.

During that first bout, I got into the habit of visiting her each week, sometimes for half an hour, sometimes for ten minutes. When she recovered, I kept coming because I enjoyed our chats and exchanges of opinion. Sometimes, when she was well or almost well, I stopped by only to find she'd gone shopping, had to take a child somewhere, or just had no time for visiting. No matter; if she was gone, I left a note and returned the next week.

We often argued—about politics for one thing, about the local church high school, for another. Sylvia felt children benefited immeasurably by going to the church school even though at that time the classes had shrunk to two or three. Although wholeheartedly in favor of our church's education, I was appalled at, among other things, the lack of social life this entailed. We agreed to disagree.

We often discussed our children, hers, young to young-adult, mine, now mostly grown, sharing what seemed to work, what didn't. And as we talked, no matter how serious the problem, the ridiculous side of it bubbled to the surface. Sylvia would throw back her head to give that gurgling laugh, I'd grimace wryly, and we'd agree that raising children, whether four or ten, would either keep you sane or complete one's mental disintegration.

The cancer returned.

There was more chemo, and this time it seemed to make her sicker. I read to her. A friend had sent *Little Tree*, a lovely, heart-wrenching story about an orphaned boy living with his grandparents, and though at first I questioned the appropriateness of reading this tale to a mother who might well be taking leave of ten children, we both soon became absorbed, reveling in the story's humor and inventiveness.

We'd both grown up in a church that spoke of the life after death as matter of factly as tomorrow's breakfast. Both she and I had absorbed Swedenborg's accounts of heaven and hell with our first solid food, but, though we spoke often of religion, we seldom mentioned death, unless obliquely. It was as though Sylvia was concentrating all her energies on staying in this world, on remaining with her husband and children as long as she could.

When Sylvia could no longer do office work, she trained others into the intricacies of the business's files and billing systems. She still commanded the life of the house, but now her headquarters was the king-size bed in the downstairs front bedroom. Each day after school the children would troop down the book lined hallway to the bedroom.

"What's for snacks?"

"There's fruit in the box beside the refrigerator."

"Can I play at Heather's?"

"Is your homework done?"

There were stays at the hospital, fortunately none of them long, and there came a time when she needed blood transfusions fairly regularly. You could tell. She'd become a little whifflery, her mind a little less sharp, and off she'd go for a transfusion, returning with her cheeks rosy red, her thought processes as incisive as ever.

"Remind me to argue with you before you have your transfusion," I said. "I like the advantage it gives me."

Was she always courageous? Damn near. Once they kept her waiting at the hospital for a procedure all afternoon and far into the night. For some reason no one would or could tell her why there was a delay or what was happening. She cried when she told me about it the next day. "No one came," she said, tears streaking her cheeks. "I was all alone, and no one would tell me anything." I held her then, and I cried too.

When she came home that time it wasn't to the king-size bed but to a hospital bed set up in the dining room. Friends came from half a country away to laugh, to share, to say goodbye. And Duncan continued somehow, no longer just husband and father, but nurse and scheduler and, like the rest of us, a helpless watcher, a bystander at the scene of an ongoing accident.

Not long before she died, I returned from a trip. Sylvia was short of breath, so I did most of the talking, giving a mini-travelogue as I sat by her bed. When I mentioned Lucerne, she said she'd been to Switzerland, years before. Had I seen the covered bridge over the river?

Yes, I'd walked through it.

She often thought of that bridge, she said. Dying must be much like that. Going through darkness into sunlight.

Another time, closer still to the trip she was about to make through her covered bridge, she said softly, "Who will explain the kids to Duncan? That's what *I've* always done. He's great with them, but I'm the one who translates for him. How will he manage?"

"I don't know," I said, "but he'll do it. Because he has to."

"Yes," she said.

And he did. In the years after her death, when I sometimes dropped by with the cookies or the homemade bread Sylvia could no longer make for her family, I marveled at just how well they all were managing. I looked at the kids sprawled on the floor doing homework, the dog trying to gnaw through someone's sock, as Duncan was cooking up a pot of spaghetti in the kitchen, and I thought "Sylvia, I think Duncan has learned to translate."

Duncan is lonely of course, but he gets by, plowing ahead with the dogged determination that has always been one of his chief qualities. When their first son was married, it was a celebration of joy for all our community. A good many wept when Duncan presented the young couple with a copy of Swedenborg's book on marriage and told them it was from both him and Sylvia.

I remember Sylvia with joy. I feel her presence often. When I look at her life, I see an amazing amalgam. I see incredible challenges met with courage and with grace. I see a life laced with large helpings of delight and several dollops of great sorrow. I see steadfastness that never gave in to despair and a sense of humor that made the very air crackle with fun and gaiety. If I look at it in the puny terms of time and space, it seems a life cut short, but if I step back a pace, I see that it was a life lived to its fullest in what was a remarkable preparation for the life to come.

NAOMI SMITH's creative nonfiction has appeared in publications as varied as *The Christian Science Monitor, Interludes* (an inflight magazine), and *The Journal of the American Medical Association.*

KATE GLEASON

The Only Love That Lasts

Who says we remember love
not as the face of the one who stays
loyal as a mirror, year after year,
but as the faces of ones who got away,
the ones who broke our hearts hard,
leaving us with an ache of consonants
like the crunch of snow, inexplicable
as Russian words, but filling us
with the pleasure of their sound?
Who says we don't want a happy love life,
don't want a steady thing, a marriage
fixed and regular as a washing machine,
its *rubba-dub-dub* replicating the heart,
the *lub-dub* heard by an infant in the womb?

Who says what we want is unrequited
love, the only love that lasts?
Myself, I want to have the cake
of love, and eat it too. I want to love
like there's no tomorrow, want to save
for the future. I want the wild, imposssible
boy who made love to me on Kerouac's grave
to be the same, comfortable husband
who throws his arm around me in sleep
as if it's a breakwater and I'm the open
sea. I want to grow to look alike

in the grand tradition of great marriages,
want our faces to wrinkle like wax paper
that's been used and smoothed and used again.

And the ones who got away? The ones
who sent me letters from foreign countries
in blue envelopes with exotic stamps,
the dark waves of ink that canceled them?
What would I want with them now, the loves
that passed like weather fronts, inconsistent
as clouds, the ones who couldn't love me
except from a distance, and only as much
as they could fit on a postcard,
the underside of too beautiful
a view, places called *Down Under* or *Great Barrier Reef?*

What would I do now with the one who left me
for Buddha, his life reduced to a single bowl?
Or the one who left so often, the pattern worn thin
on the rug by my door, the roses gone
threadbare, left to the imagination?
Back when love seemed to happen
only on a grand scale. Back when it seemed
love had to enter me the way an ocean
thunders into the hollow of a shell,
and then recedes, in order to leave its song.

KATE GLEASON is the author of two collections of poetry: *Making As If to Sing* and *The Brighter the Deeper.* Her work has also appeared in *Best American Poetry, Green Mountains Review, Sonora Review, The Spoon River Poetry Review, Midland Review, Sojourner, The Anthology of Magazine Verse and Yearbook of American Poetry,* and *Claiming the Spirit Within.* Formerly the editor of *Peregrine* literary journal and a Poet-in-the-Schools, she currently teaches creative writing workshops in southern New Hampshire.

ERNEST MILLS

The Dream Barn

Dorris Lee. *Helicopter.* Oil on canvas, 42 × 28 inches, 1943. Tucson: The University of Arizona Museum of Art. Gift of Mr. and Mrs. Vernon Newell. 69.14.1.

SHORTLY AFTER THE TURN OF THE CENTURY,' my grandfather and his family moved to Milton, Indiana, where grandfather pastored the Quaker meeting. My father, then living on a farm in nearby Henry County, went to Milton to attend the commencement of his sister's graduation. A beautiful, tall, young woman gave the leading oration. As father sat in the audience, he vowed to himself that some day he would marry that woman. And so he did in 1906. In the meantime, father sold his farm and bought 40 acres a half-mile south of the Hopewell Friends meeting house and brought his young bride with him.

My mother reminisced how she came with father to their newly purchased farm:

One cold, rainy morning in April, Roy and I started on our wedding journey. In an open buggy, we drove nine miles to our small home. It was in total chaos and disrepair. We put in long hours from morning to night to make it more liveable and plant the crops.

The house was so small, it had to be cut in two parts, moving the front end of the building out to the west eight feet, thus creating an opening for additional space between the two parts. The fences were falling down and overgrown with poison vines and weeds, debris everywhere. In a few weeks, we cleared out most of the accumulation of rubbish and soon old-fashioned flowers softened the rest. Sunshine, fresh air, and blue sky began to buoy up our spirits. Hope for the future brightened.

While Roy was busy outside with spring work, I was busy inside varnishing, painting, and cleaning. We bought a few goods, rugs, curtains, and pieces of furniture that changed the small domain into a fairy palace to our eyes.

There were hired men to cook for no matter how hot the days were. Water had to be carried from a well at the barn. Brooding hens squawked at me when I passed by, and cross bees entangled themselves in my hair whenever I went to the orchard for fruit.

We did not find time to make a garden in the daytime, so I followed Roy up and down the rows with a smoky lantern while he dropped the seeds. Our neighbors were curious as to what we were doing and said we should plant by the light of the moon if we expect a crop. But, to their surprise, the vegetables flourished.

I WAS BORN AT HOME IN 1917. My father made a frantic dash to town with a horse and buggy to get the doctor. Years later, while visiting the corporate offices in Florida of the company I worked for, some of the girls asked me if I had always lived in that old house. I told them I live in the same house on the same farm and sleep in the same bed where I was born. They all burst out laughing.

My youth was shadowed by the Great Depression of the 1930s. Mere existence required the total labor of our entire family. Father struggled to keep bread on the table, clothes on our backs, and pay the farm mortgage, mostly interest.

I remember in those days I started working before sunrise, first bringing in the milk cows from the barn half a mile away behind the farm, then cleaning and harnessing the horses before breakfast for the field work. We did the milking by hand. Father was much better than I at that; he could milk ten cows while I only five.

My father, a tender and compassionate person, only whipped me once. As a little boy, I was sent to the strawberry patch to pick berries for breakfast. I brought in a box full—about half of them green. He ordered me to go back out and pick a box of ripe berries this time. When I returned with another box of partly green berries, he thought that I had deliberately done this and whipped me. When I was about twenty years old, we planted seven acres of tomatoes for the canning factory. On the first load which I had picked and hauled to town, the government agent graded the load about 40 percent culls (too green). He gave me a color-chart test for color blindness and advised me to stay away from picking tomatoes. Coming home and reporting to dad that I was color-blind, tears came to his eyes. He reached out and embraced me, saying, "To think I whipped you as a little boy for picking green strawberries."

My mother, like all rural women, had a hard life. She heated the wash water in a copper boiler on top of the cook stove. We devised a way to have soft water for doing the laundry by directing the water from the eaves and downspouts into a cistern. It was my job to fill the copper boiler and the reservoir tank on the side of the wood-burning cookstove.

Mother also took care of the chickens. We usually kept 100 laying hens, and to get them, she had to set broody hens. Keeping hens on the eggs until they hatched (about 21 days) was a chore. Then we had the little chickens to take care of. Truly, "Man's work is from sun to sun, but woman's work is never done."

In the fall, mother made apple butter in a huge copper kettle that had been in the family for generations. She peeled the apples, sliced and cooked them over an open fire, stirring with a wooden paddle, being careful not to let the apple butter burn. She also made soap at this time, having set aside the rancid lard and leftover bacon grease throughout the year. Adding lye, she boiled the lard and grease in an iron kettle, creating a beautiful, white soap.

THE SEASON GOVERNED OUR WORK. In the springtime, gardens were made, potatoes planted, and strawberries harvested. We had thirty fruit trees and twenty bee hives. We extracted the honey and bucketed ten half-gallon cans for the honey market. By this time, grain was hauled to the mill to be ground for feed for chickens, hogs, and cows. There was also the weekly hauling of manure from the hen house and barn. We plowed the land for the corn crop with a walking plow, plowing two acres a day with two horses. In preparation for corn planting, we leveled the ground by pulling a drag and running a harrow. I used to hate every click of the seed going into the ground for I knew it represented an ear of corn that had to be husked and harvested by hand that fall. Life moved in a never-ending cycle. No sooner did we get the corn plowed, than it was time to do the haying. We mowed, raked, and pitched the hay, hauled it to the barn by wagon, and pulled it up into the mow with a hay fork and rope.

After haymaking, we would try to get another cultivation of corn, and a third cultivation if possible. By now, we were in the wheat field using a wheat binder—an interesting event to me because the binder was the only piece of mechanized equipment on the farm. It cut the wheat, tied it into bundles, and dropped it off in rows to be stood up in shocks to dry out for threshing.

Threshing was also an important time for the women. The men would finish up at one farm in the morning and move on to the next at lunch time. The women would go down the road and prepare the meal, usually chicken and pies, to feed the hungry threshing gang. The men were fed in the dining room. Sometimes an extra table might be set up. The first ten men in would eat while the rest of the crew waited for their turn outside. Washing dishes, setting tables, were also the chores of the women.

By August, it was time to fill the silos. We cut the green corn—ears, stalk, and all—with a corn binder, hauled it in on wagons, threw it in the chopper, and blew it up into the silo.

By early in October, corn husking began. We went down through the field, a man taking two rows at a time, husking the corn by hand, and throwing it into a wagon which followed along with a team of horses. This tedious chore lasted into November, hopefully not past Christmas. Any farmer who had corn out after Christmas was considered a poor farmer.

During the winter, we spent most of our Saturdays in the woods with crosscut saw and ax, cutting wood to keep the house warm. Our heat was generated by a one-register cast iron furnace. In the basement, I fed this furnace big chunks of wood. That grate upstairs was so hot it seemed that you had to burn your feet to get warm!

This was our yearly cycle, to say nothing about caring for little pigs and lambs which arrived, repairing fences, graveling the lane, fixing the drain, picking fruits, spraying the orchard, and pruning the trees.

It was not uncommon, especially in the winter, to be in the field until dark doing our farm chores and milking the cows in the barn by lantern light. We never went to bed until all the livestock had been fed and watered and cared for. Father used to tell me, "Treat your milk cow as you would treat your mother." He loved his milk cows, and wouldn't allow them to be abused in any way.

Although dad didn't have much money, he made improvements whenever he could. He bought an old, International upright gas engine and installed it on the back porch. The engine was about four feet high. With a series of belts and jack-shafts overhead, he ran power to mother's antique washing machine, the cream separator, and the well pump.

EVENTUALLY, I LEFT HOME and went to Earlham College. Being a Quaker, it was a natural choice and proved to be a great experience. As a freshman, I made the school's varsity baseball team, and we were undefeated throughout my sophomore year. I made several lifelong friends at Earlham. Since then I have served on the board of trustees.

I came home from college to a different world. In my absence, electricity had been brought to the farm by the Rural Electrification Administration. There were electric lights, and mother now had an electric cook stove. She had running water and a good washing machine powered by electricity. She had an electric iron and got rid of the flat irons. She often said that having electricity on the farm made her twenty years younger.

I had come home to a brand-new, shiny Massey–Harris tractor with steel wheels. It had a two-row corn plow mounted on it with a power lift. You would come to the end of the row and just hit a little button with your heel, the plow raised up, and you drove around the end rows, hit the button again, and plowed another row. This was a great improvement.

We now made hay with a hay baler, and we no longer threshed. The combine had replaced the wheat binder and the threshing machine. Gravel came by commercial truck, and we got rid of the bees. The old orchard trees died off. The world of farming had suddenly become more interesting and fun, no longer hard labor and endless chores.

Shortly after World War II, I got married and went into farming. The farm I had was adjacent to my parents' place, a beautiful farm of 120 acres with good ground, but no barn. I wanted to milk the dairy cows my father had raised, so I went to the woods with a hired man and a cross cut saw. We cut down 25 trees, had them sawed up into dimension lumber, and built a new, beautiful 36-by-60 barn. I built most of it with my own hands—it took two years, 2000 pounds of nails, and 3000 hours of my labor.

The new barn was a grade-A dairy barn. We no longer milked cows by hand, but had an automatic milker and an electric cooler to keep the milk fresh. I milked cows for four or five years and had the best dairy herd in the county, but the old itch of driving huge bull-dozers and earth movers was too much for me. I couldn't plow another row of corn or feed another hog. I had to have some big machinery. So I bought three Caterpillar tractors and went into the earth-moving business.

With this equipment, I built a lot of farm ponds, two big dams, roads, and leveled building sites for commercial homes and new industry. Doing the building site for Standard Dry Wall Products in Centerville led to a new career as regional salesman and, eventually, as the company's technical advisor. I traveled the world for many years on the company's behalf to Europe, Saudi Arabia, New Zealand, Australia, and Singapore. As a farm boy, I would dream each year of going the fifty miles to the Indiana State Fair. As it turned out, I traveled a lot farther than that.

IN 1983, WE BUILT A HOME ON THE KNOLL across the road from the old family place. My parents had hoped to build their new home here. My mother always liked this spot. As a matter of fact, our source of water is taken from the very well they dug to supply their home-to-be. But the top of the old farmhouse burned, and mother and dad used their savings to rebuild.

Our passive solar home, which we call Five Oaks, is located in the middle of the woods I frequented as a boy. In the early fall, we found good pawpaws there to eat. Roots of a weeping willow had dammed up the creek that ran through the back of the woods, forming a swimming hole. Between chores in the summer, I would slip over there and take a dip. The trees are mostly gone now, but there is the shade of a big beech tree which I used to climb. I can look out over the spring fields, soon to be under cultivation. Across the road, the old farm house, barn, and outbuildings are still standing. You can yet make out the edges of the clay tennis court father and I built years ago on the south side of the driveway. On Sunday afternoons, many neighbor boys and girls would come to our farm to play. We played baseball, tennis, croquet, and horseshoes. My parents felt the neighborhood needed some kind of activity for the young people. It was like a private park, but it was more than that, you never knew who might drop by.

One Sunday at noon, an airplane flew very low over the house and barn. We all rushed outside to see because an airplane was an oddity in those days. The plane landed in the big hay field and taxied up to the barn. The motor shut down, and we all hurried over to get a better look. It was an old, two-seater Jenny of World War I vintage. The aviator and another man got out. They explained that they were en route to Indianapolis and had decided to land to avoid flying into major turbulence coming up in the west. We invited them into the house. Mother had a good noon meal on the table. The pilot turned out to be Colonel Roscoe Turner, a famous speed flier, three-time winner of the Thompson Trophy, and record-holder of transcontinental flights. Turner was a national hero. He was known to stroll down Los Angeles streets resplendent in his blue tunic, brown breeches, Sam Browne belt, and knee-high boots. It was not uncommon for him to be seen with a parachute draped over one shoulder and his pet lion Gilmore on a leash. After dinner, Colonel Turner asked to take a nap and made himself comfortable on the living room couch. After a couple of hours, our guests climbed into their open cockpit, took off, and continued their journey. It was an occasion that I will always remember, just like so many other memories of my growing years that will forever linger in my mind.

The reminiscences of ERNEST MILLS were tape recorded before his death and transcribed by Robert Lawson and his daughter, Rebecca Skinner Lawson, members of the Hopewell Friends Meeting.

Afterwords

THE CONCLUDING PIECES THAT FOLLOW SPEAK for themselves. But something more needs to be said about the preceding introductions to the four parts of this volume. The
process and goal of *Becoming New,* briefly suggested in these
single pages, are developed into a comprehensive teaching by
Emanuel Swedenborg. Readers interested to follow more
deeply into the system will find it developed from a base of
biblical imagery in paragraphs 1 to 72 of the first volume of
Swedenborg's *Arcana Coelestia* (available singly in paper or
hard cover from the Swedenborg Foundation), and more
theoretically elsewhere in Swedenborg's works.

Published editions of *Arcana Coelestia* [sometimes
translated as *Heavenly Secrets*] and other books by
Swedenborg offer a different vocabulary than I have used in
these introductions. What I have translated "becoming new"
appears as "regeneration"; my "turning around" is rendered
"repentance"; and "changing ourselves" reads as "reforma-
tion." With this difference, the *Arcana* and other Swedenborg
sources provide a priceless self-improvement guide, a psychological and spiritual handbook to the good life.

—ROBERT H. KIRVEN
INTRODUCTIONS EDITOR

ALICE B. SKINNER

A Cosmic Quality

Beauty surrounds us: a myrtle warbler perches for a moment on the golden forsythia bush, lilacs circulate their arresting aroma, the haunting song of the hermit thrush echoes through the woods.

> The heavens declare God's glory
> and the magnificence of what made them.
> Each new dawn is a miracle;
> each new sky fills with beauty.[1]

Beauty takes many forms. People—painters, home makers, musicians—create wonders of color and symmetry, inspiring eye and spirit. A writer finds beauty in a person:

> She had that indefinable beauty that comes from happpiness, enthusiasm, success—a beauty that is nothing more or less than a harmony of temperament and circumstances.[2]

Andrew Wyeth. *Maga's Daughter.* Tempera, 30 × 26½ inches, 1966. Private collection.

Beauty may be heard in music and found in abstract ideas:

Facts which at first seem improbable
will, even on scant explanation,
drop the cloak which has hidden them
and stand forth in naked and simple beauty.

Mathematics, rightly viewed,
possesses not only truth
but supreme beauty;—
a beauty cold and austere,
like that of sculpture.[3]

Hans Poelzig. *Study for a Concert Hall, Salzburg Festival, Salzburg, Austria, Interior Perspective.* Colored pencil and pencil on tracing paper, 16³/16 × 14⁵/8 inches, 1918. New York: The Museum of Modern Art. Gift of Henry G. Proshauer. Photograph ©1997, New York: The Museum of Modern Art.

What converts everyday observations into beauty?

Things are pretty, graceful, rich, elegant, handsome, but until
they speak to the imagination, not yet beautiful. . . . The new
virtue which constitutes a thing beautiful, is a certain cosmical
quality, or a power to suggest relation to the whole world
and so lift the object out of a pitiful individuality. Every
natural feature—sea, sky, rainbow, flowers, musical tone—
has in it somewhat which is not private, but universal, speaks
of that central benefit which is the soul of Nature, and thereby
is beautiful.[4]

[1] Psalm 19: 1–2.
[2] Gustave Flaubert. *Madame Bovary.* Francis Steegmuller, trans. Part II. Ch. 12.
[3] Bertrand Russell. The Study of Mathematics. *Philosophical Essays.* No. 4. 1910.
[4] Ralph Waldo Emerson. Beauty. *Essays and English Traits.* 1860.

Sakai Hoitsu. *Pond Scene with Iris and Mandarin Ducks*. Ink, color, and gold on silk, Edo Period (1615–1868), early nineteenth century. Dallas Museum of Art, Foundation for the Arts, gift of Mr. and Mrs. Stephen S. Kahn.

Beauty tutors us in meaning.

The shore is an ancient world, for as long as there has been an earth and sea there has been this place of the meeting of land and water. . . . Each time that I enter it, I gain some new awareness of its beauty and its deeper meanings, sensing the intricate fabric of life by which one creature is linked with another, and each with its surroundings . . . Underlying the beauty of the spectacle there is meaning and significance. It is the elusiveness of that meaning that haunts us, that sends us again and again into the natural world where the key to the riddle is hidden.[5]

And nurtures the spirit

A work of art, or anything that affects us
    as art does,
may truly be said to do something to us . . .
it clarifies and organizes intuition itself . . .
In art, it is the impact of the whole,
the immediate revelation of vital import,
that acts as the psychological lure
to long contemplation.[6]

And invites happiness

Swedenborg says all happinesses flow into beauty. To be distinctly one's own person, doing what one longs to do because of the innate delight of the Lord's love in one, is happiness that must shine and flow into beauty.[7]

[5] Rachel Carson. *The Edge of the Sea*. Boston: Houghton Mifflin Company. 1955. pp. 2, 7.
[6] Susanne K. Langer. *Feeling and Form*. New York: Charles Scribner's Sons 1953. p. 397.
[7] Alice Archer Sewall James. *The Garden Gate*. Letters based on the writings of Emanuel Swedenborg. Unpublished manuscript in the Archives of the Swedenborg School of Religion, Newton, Massachusetts. Paragraph 506.

Beauty is the gift of God.[8]

Nothing beautiful and charming exists
in the heavens or on earth;
that does not by some relationship
portray the Lord's kingdom.[9]

Into every beautiful object,
there enters somewhat immeasurable and divine,
and just as much into form bounded by outlines,
like mountains on the horizon,
as into tones of music or depths of space.
Polarized light showed the secret architecture of bodies;
and when the *second-sight* of the mind is opened,
now one color or form or gesture, and now another,
has a pungency, as if a more interior ray had been emitted,
disclosing its deep holdings in the frame of things.[10]

William Trost Richards.
*The Franconia
Mountains from
Compton, New
Hampshire.* Watercolor,
$14^{3}/_{16} \times 8^{3}/_{16}$ inches,
1872. New York: The
Metroplitan Museum of
Art. Gift of Reverend
Elias L. Magoon, 1880.
80.1.5

8 Aristotle. In Diogenes Laaertius. *Aristotle.* Book V. Sec. 19.
9 Emanuel Swedenborg. *Arcana Coelestia.* George Dole, trans. 1807.
10 Ralph Waldo Emerson. Op. cit.

Beauty transforms us:

Beautiful my desire, and the place of my desire.
I think of the rock singing, and light making its own silence
At the edge of a ripening meadow, in early summer.
Near this rose, in this grove of sun-parched, wind-warped
madronas
Among the half-dead trees, I came upon the true ease of myself,
As if another man appeared out of the depths of my being,
And I stood outside myself,
Beyond becoming and perishing,
A something wholly other,
As if I swayed out on the wildest wave alive,
And yet was still.
And I rejoiced in being what I was . . .[11]

William Blake.
*Songs of Innocence
and of Experience.*
Frontispiece. Relief
etching with pen
and watercolor, 1789.
New Haven: Yale Center
for British Art, Paul
Mellon Collection.

[11]Theodore Roethke. *The Collected Poems.* New York: Doubleday, Anchor Books. 1975.
pp. 198–199.

ALICE B. SKINNER, president of the Swedenborg Foundation, looks for beauty in art and poetry to share with those who treasure the Chrysalis Reader.

WILSON VAN DUSEN

Cosmic Good

IN CHINESE TAOISM, the real order of existence is called the tao. It is wisdom and, out of that, happiness to come into harmony with the way things are. In so doing the individual discovers that even inwardly one is already part of this order. Most of the examples given of tao describe a play of opposites, yin and yang, male and female, light and dark. But lest one suspect these opposites are only in the created realm, there is also a Taoistic Buddhism that carries these opposites through all fields of existence. The essential pattern here is that there is an order to existence, and we would do well to discover it and come into harmony with what is.

There is a parallel to taoism in the works of the western mystic Emanuel Swedenborg. He describes existence as in a given order,

Giovanni del Biondo. Italian. *Vision of St. Benedict.* Tempera and gold leaf on panel, 39.3 × 35.8 cm, fourteenth century. Toronto: Art Gallery of Ontario. Gift of A.L. Koppel, 1953.

which includes ourselves. Wisdom, or good, and the highest happiness arise out of perceiving this order and then choosing to live in harmony with it. Since individuals are a microcosm, or a miniature universe, this cosmic order includes the very design of our own nature. So—harmony with the nature of the whole of existence, and harmony with our own inner nature are the same thing. Each good person is a miniature heaven, or a church in the least form.

But now I feel a great challenge. How to describe this cosmic order that took Swedenborg decades in the spiritual worlds to discover? It is challenging to describe because we are dealing with a comprehensive image that includes everything. First let us journey to the spiritual worlds beyond this life for a look at the most comprehensive image.

Ultimately only God, the Lord, exists. This is a grand insight that can be found in Hindu Advaita Vedanta, Buddhism, Christianity, and in Islam. This poses an immediate problem. What is all the rest of existence, ourselves, and nature then? All the rest of existence are representations of the divine. When seen well, the divine chooses to show its nature as creation. Creation is then a correspondent or a representation, or an image of the whole. Of course this applies to us also. In one way our body, as a remarkable assemblage of parts all serving our life, is an image of what Swedenborg describes as the Grand Human of heaven. The Grand Human of heaven is a representation of the life of God as composed of various parts and aspects that are the societies of heaven all directed to one divine end. Indeed my own experiences of heaven were overwhelmingly of a unified enlightened society in a communal unity of work toward one end. And what is that end? It is enunciated in the Eastern Orthodox Church as the salvation of all, of everyone, and everything. And what really is salvation in this sense? It is that all return into its ultimate nature, God. This ultimate design is best described in Swedenborg's *Heaven and Hell*.[1]

But let us step down from this ultimate design nearer to our situation. Our innermost design is exactly that of heaven. We are made in the image. The Lord streams forth as the sun of heaven. This sun is apparent to angels. It is the spiritual correspondent of our earthly sun. But in heaven it always is the east where it represents the dawning awareness of those living in the love and wisdom of God. The divine sun streams forth divine love and wisdom to be received at each level of creation according to its capacity to receive. This divine love in wisdom is the very source of our inner life. Life is given to us. We are recipient vessels. The very nature and quality of our inner life depends upon how we receive this.

Part of the very design of this life given to us, moment by moment, is that we are to feel ourselves as free and independent agents.

So, as free agents we can construe this design, which we are, any way we please. We can fantasy that we are God, and rule the universe, though most perceptive people would soon see this is not true. We get, and ultimately are, according to how we receive and use this life given to us. The good person matures into one who sees his or her effect on others and is affected in turn by others. Good persons comes to see they are merely a local phenomenon in the larger fabric of existence. The Buddhist idea of dependent origination fits in here. We are dealing with a single fabric of existence in which all are interdependent and part of the One Life.

In our ultimate freedom we can construe our existence in any way that pleases us. The criminal suspects all are crooks, and it is a dog-eat-dog world. Grab what you can. Each of the many ways of turning against the one fabric of existence, towards *me first,* automatically constricts our existence. The person who grabs for *me first* is not able to experience the simple joy of heaven, of being part of a greater whole. The for-myself-first existence constricts and darkens experience and various aspects of this are described by Swedenborg as hell. Swedenborg was criticized because the hell he described was too automatic, the simple result of poor choices. No God punished. It was self-chosen and self-designed and thereby automatic. The different societies of hell simply reflected different kinds of for-themselves choices.

But let us look more closely at the possibilities for the good person who comes to sense himself as a part of the very fabric of existence. The welfare of the whole becomes uppermost. Along this path she discovers what Swedenborg described as her life's love. I know nowhere else in the world's literature where this is so clearly brought out. The life's love is an innermost tendency that was given by God to the individual. It is the very essence of individuality. It is the uniqueness of the person. It is also what the person can do best, and where he or she can be of the greatest use to the whole. Because it is the essence of one's love, acting in it the person also senses the greatest freedom, the freedom to do what one loves. So, in short, operating in the general thesis that we are a part of the whole fabric of existence, we also discover our innermost nature and where we are designed to be of the greatest use, both to ourselves and to the fabric of existence as a whole. This, of course, prepares us for a society in heaven where we join kindred spirits working toward similar ends. The ideal life on earth prepares us for heaven. Heaven is not so far off. It is the inner and ultimate aspect of the good life here.

So, then, what is cosmic good, good conceived in its most ultimate aspect? It begins with using our life to its best use, to discover the ultimate nature of reality. Since it is written both in ourselves and in the very order of events, it is not so remote. We meet it everyday.

Every religious tradition tries in its own way to lead to it. Our innermost love of life is a natural path we can trod easier than any other. It is an in-built path to the Source of Life itself.

But having begun to perceive something of the harmonious design of the whole, the good person chooses to come into harmony with it. There is a natural drift in us toward this. But this also leads into the highest delights that can be known in this world. We were commissioned out of God and there is much in the very nature and design of things that leads us back to God.

Do we thereby lose ourselves in God? No. Swedenborg makes quite clear that the more fully we choose to act in harmony with the order of existence the more fully and freely do we seem to be ourselves.[2] Actually, the journey from the little fretful self to becoming a part of all there is, is a vast expansion. The prodigal son, who wandered so far from home, is welcomed home.

The basic wisdom of this design is really apparent. If existence, all existence including my innermost self, is in a given design, I best discover it and come into harmony with it. This is especially true if I thereby come into my own highest uses and simultaneously the greatest joys a person can know. The Way is remarkably well marked by joy. But there is also another benefit in this way of cosmic good. Those who choose to join with the universal design of it all, are allowed to see into the whole design. This accounts for Swedenborg's unusual insights. Why is this so? If you are a voluntary part of the universal order, you are already living in this order. From living to perceiving is an easy step. Common examples of this are those of various sacred traditions who suddenly perceive great depth in their own sacred scriptures. This comes about because those who strive for harmony with the order of existence thereby open up their interior into higher spiritual realms. Swedenborg uses the term conjunction instead of harmony. Conjunction means literally what is joined. What we are joined with we more easily perceive.

The ultimate or cosmic good for us humans arises when we perceive the real order of existence, and choose to join with it, and become a part of it. We are thereby expanded into the largest life and joy we can know.

WILSON VAN DUSEN is a clinical psychologist and author of numerous books on the inner world.

Notes

1. E. Swedenborg, *Heaven and Hell.* West Chester, Pennsylvania: Swedenborg Foundation. I highly recommend the shorter *Heaven and Hell* as covering the same ground in an easier format. It is also available from the Foundation.

2. Emanuel Swedenborg. *Divine Providence.* Paragraph 158. (In Swedenborgian studies it is customary to cite paragraph numbers rather than page numbers since the paragraph numbers are uniform in all editons and translations of Swedenborg's works).

JAN FRAZIER

Meteor Shower Party

We met in a round black meadow under the stars,
forecast to burst across the August infinite
like Independence Night. People knew the hosts
only, each other not at all. As if to force
the strangers to feel for one another,
a blanket of clouds slid between meteors
and lookers. Noses and chins lowered:
Who are you? I wonder what you look like.
We had to creep close, smell
a stranger's breath. There was laughter, here and there
a loud, forlorn sigh about the cloud cover.
A telescope stood absurd sentinel.

By silent consent, we settled into anonymity,
relieved to not have a name
for each unfeatured face. We were voices
floating over the grass under the clouds,
coming close, moving apart, a dance
of the disembodied. A woman's voice
spoke of a UFO hovering
above a farm in Wisconsin
twenty years before. A deeper voice
told the story of a friend' funeral.
A small snore fluttered up from a mound
of blankets on the soft, dewy grass.

Jean Francois Millet. *Starry Night.* Oil on canvas, mounted on wood, 32⅛ × 25¾ inches, ca. 1851. New Haven, Connecticut: Yale University Art Gallery. Leonard C. Hanna Jr. B.A. 1913, Fund.

Someone piled up firewood, threw on a match.
The orange flames held our eyes, kept us faceless.
The silhouettes of young boys drew near the fire,
torched marshmellows at the ends of sticks.
A voice cool and sweet like juice sang *Good Night, Irene.*
When it finished, there was not a sound in the meadow
but the spit and crack of the wood giving up its soul.
A man said softly, "Again." And she sang it
once more. By the time she got through to
"I'll see you in my dreams," we had all joined in,
one by one coming along with her,
a choir of blind and solitary voices.

JAN FRAZIER's poetry has appeared in *Passages North, Yankee Magazine, The Plum Review, Minnesota Review, Christian Science Monitor,* and other journals and anthologies. She is a Pushcart Prize nominee and the recipient of a commendation in the National Poetry Competion of the Chester H. Jones Foundation.